Standard Grade | General

Biology

General Level 2003
_____

General Level 2004
_____

General Level 2005
_____

General Level 2006
_____

General Level 2007
_____

First exam published in 2003.
Published by Leckie & Leckie Ltd, 3rd Floor, 4 Queen Street, Edinburgh EH2 1JE
tel: 0131 220 6831 fax: 0131 225 9987 enquiries@leckieandleckie.co.uk www.leckieandleckie.co.uk

ISBN 978-1-84372-500-8

A CIP Catalogue record for this book is available from the British Library.

Printed in Scotland by Scotprint.

Leckie & Leckie is a division of Huveaux plc.

Leckie & Leckie is grateful to the copyright holders, as credited at the back of the book, for permission to use their material.
Every effort has been made to trace the copyright holders and to obtain their permission for the use of copyright material.
Leckie & Leckie will gladly receive information enabling them to rectify any error or omission in subsequent editions.

2003 | General

[BLANK PAGE]

G

KU	PS

Total Marks

0300/401

NATIONAL
QUALIFICATIONS
2003

MONDAY 26 MAY
9.00 AM – 10.30 AM

BIOLOGY
STANDARD GRADE
General Level

Fill in these boxes and read what is printed below.

Full name of centre

Town

Forename(s)

Surname

Date of birth
Day Month Year   Scottish candidate number   Number of seat

1 All questions should be attempted.

2 The questions may be answered in any order but all answers are to be written in the spaces provided in this answer book, and must be written clearly and legibly in ink.

3 Rough work, if any should be necessary, as well as the fair copy, is to be written in this book. Additional spaces for answers and for rough work will be found at the end of the book. Rough work should be scored through when the fair copy has been written.

4 Before leaving the examination room you must give this book to the invigilator. If you do not, you may lose all the marks for this paper.

SCOTTISH
QUALIFICATIONS
AUTHORITY

Marks | KU | PS

1. The diagram gives some information about a woodland in southern Scotland.

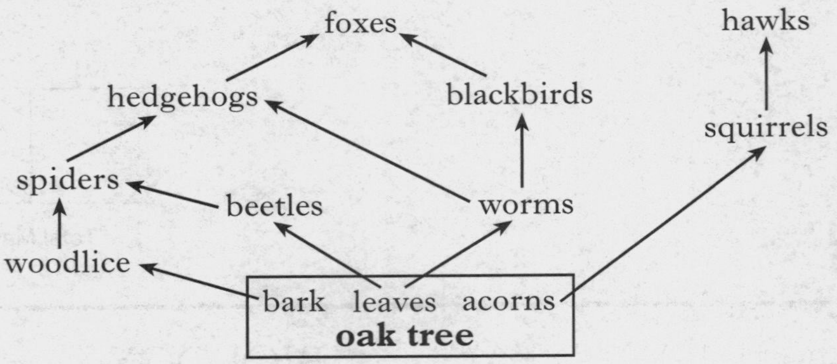

(a) What name is given to this type of diagram?

_____   **1**

(b) Answer the following using information **from the diagram**.

(i) Name **one** producer and **one** consumer.

Producer _____   Consumer _____   **1**

(ii) What do the arrows in the diagram represent?

_____   **1**

(iii) Complete the food chain below.

oak leaves ⟶ _____ ⟶ _____ ⟶ _____ ⟶ foxes   **1**

(iv) Name the part of the oak tree not involved in the food chains that include foxes.

_____   **1**

(v) Which part of the oak tree provides energy for the greatest number of different species?

_____   **1**

(c) Complete the table of words about the biosphere and their meanings.

Word	Meaning
habitat	
	all the animals or plants of a single species living in an area
	a particular area and all the animals and plants which live there

3

KU | PS

Marks | KU | PS

2. The table shows the mass of some of the main air pollutants produced in Britain in one year.

Pollutant	Mass produced (tonnes per year)
sulphur dioxide	4000
dust and grit	1500
carbon monoxide	6000
smoke	1000
others	500
TOTAL	

(a) Complete the table by entering the total mass of pollutants in the space provided.

1

(b) The pie chart below shows the information from the table.

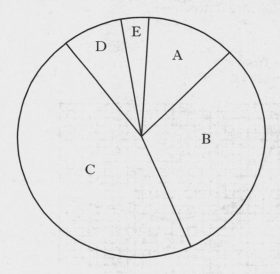

(i) Which letter represents the pollution due to dust and grit?

Letter _____

1

(ii) Identify the pollutants represented by segments C and D on the chart.

C _____

1

D _____

1

3. The graphs below show the oxygen concentrations upstream and downstream from the outflow pipes of two different sewage works, **A** and **B**. The two sewage works receive equal quantities of sewage and the two rivers are of equal size and speed.

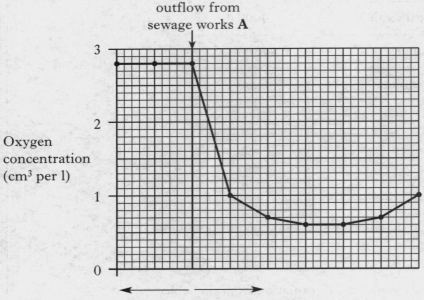

outflow from
sewage works **A**

Oxygen concentration (cm³ per l)

distance upstream   distance downstream

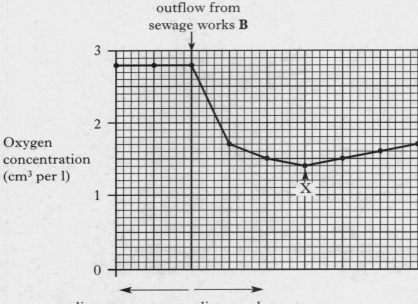

outflow from
sewage works **B**

Oxygen concentration (cm³ per l)

X

distance upstream   distance downstream

(*a*) What is the oxygen concentration of the water upstream from sewage works **A**?

_____ cm³ per l

1

DO NOT
WRITE IN
THIS
MARGIN

Marks | KU | PS

3. **(continued)**

(b) Calculate the percentage of oxygen lost from the water between the outflow of sewage works **B** and point **X**.

Space for calculation

_____ %

1

(c) Complete the following sentence to describe the change in oxygen concentration which takes place downstream from both sewage works.

As the distance downstream from the sewage works increases, the

oxygen concentration _____ and then _____ .

1

(d) Which sewage works is more efficient at removing waste material from the sewage?
Give a reason for your answer.

Sewage works _____

1

Reason _____

_____

1

(e) Give **one** example of a disease that may be spread by untreated sewage.

_____

1

[Turn over

4. The diagrams show three different types of human teeth.

A   B   C

(a) (i) Complete the following table by choosing **one** of the teeth, **A**, **B** or **C**, for each description.

Each letter may be used once, more than once or not at all.

Description of tooth	Tooth
Found at the very back of the jaw	
Known as an incisor	
Used for grinding and crushing food	

2

(ii) State **one** function of canine teeth in carnivores.

_____

_____

1

DO NOT WRITE IN THIS MARGIN

Marks	KU	PS

4. (continued)

(*b*) Fluoride can be added to water supplies to help reduce tooth decay. The following bar graph shows the results of a study into the effect of some fluoride concentrations on the decay of children's teeth.

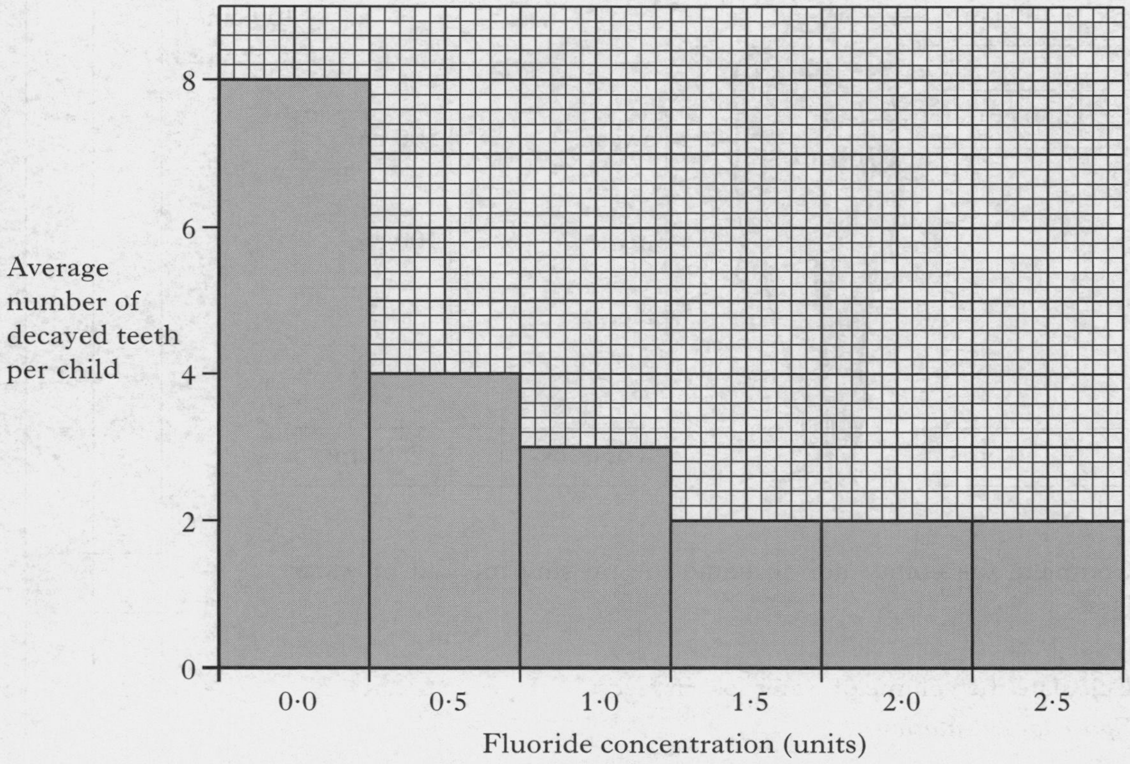

(i) What was the average number of decayed teeth per child when the fluoride concentration was 1 unit?

__________ decayed teeth per child **1**

(ii) On average, how many teeth per child were saved from decay by increasing the fluoride concentration from 0·0 to 0·5 units?

__________ teeth per child **1**

(iii) It may be concluded from the study that a fluoride concentration of 1·5 ppm is best.

Explain why this concentration would be better than each of the following.

1 1·0 unit ______________________________

____ **1**

2 2·0 units ______________________________

____ **1**

Marks | KU | PS

5. (a) The following diagram shows the main methods of water gain and loss for the human body.

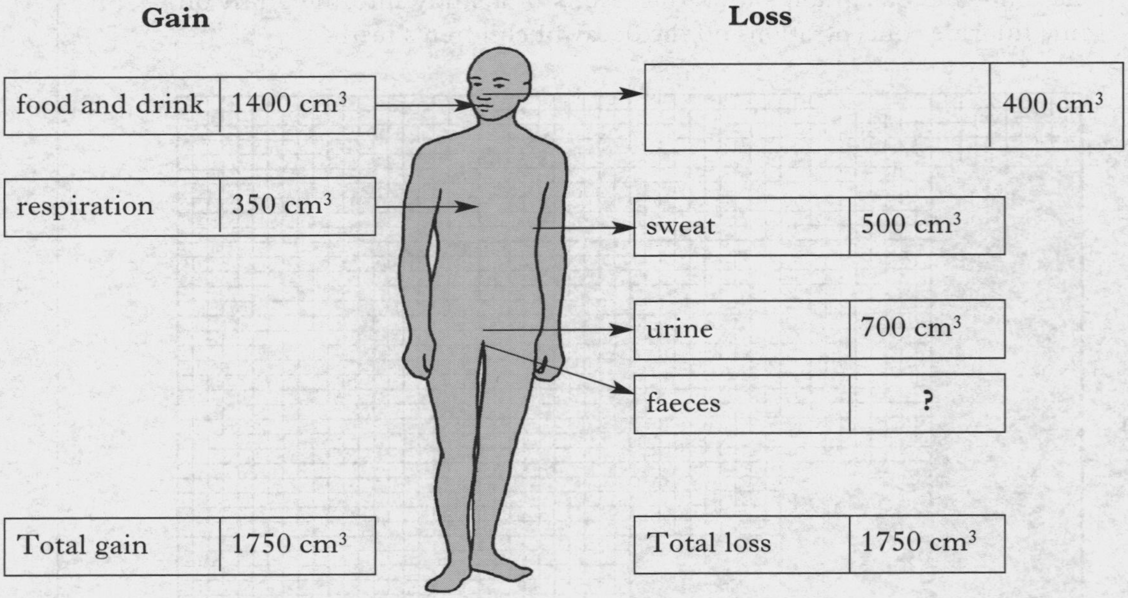

Gain

| food and drink | 1400 cm³ |

| respiration | 350 cm³ |

| Total gain | 1750 cm³ |

Loss

| | 400 cm³ |

| sweat | 500 cm³ |

| urine | 700 cm³ |

| faeces | ? |

| Total loss | 1750 cm³ |

(i) Complete the empty box to name the missing method of water loss.

1

(ii) Calculate the volume of water lost in faeces.

Space for calculation

_____ cm³

1

(iii) What percentage of the water gained comes from respiration?

Space for calculation

_____ %

1

(b) Which organs are directly responsible for regulating the water content of the blood?

_____

1

(c) Name the poisonous waste substance that is removed in the urine together with water and salts.

_____

1

5. **(continued)**

(*d*) The table shows the volumes of juices released into the digestive system each day.

Digestive juice	Volume (cm³)
saliva	1500
gastric juice	2500
bile	500
pancreatic juice	700
intestinal juice	3000

Use the table to complete the **bar chart** below by:

(i)   labelling the vertical axis   **1**

(ii)   adding the scale to the vertical axis   **1**

(iii)   completing the bars   **1**

(Additional graph paper, if required, will be found on page 27.)

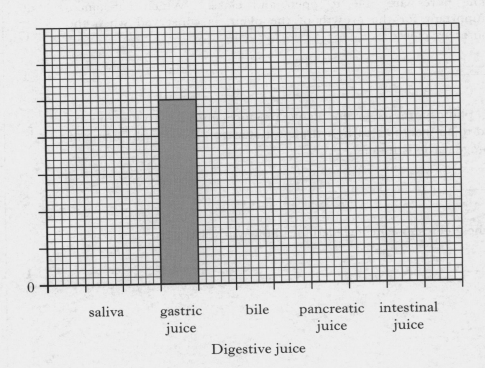

Digestive juice

(*e*) Which part of the digestive system reabsorbs most of the water from the juices?

_____   **1**

Page nine   **[Turn over**

DO NOT WRITE IN THIS MARGIN

Marks | KU | PS

6. The diagram shows the lower surface of a leaf.

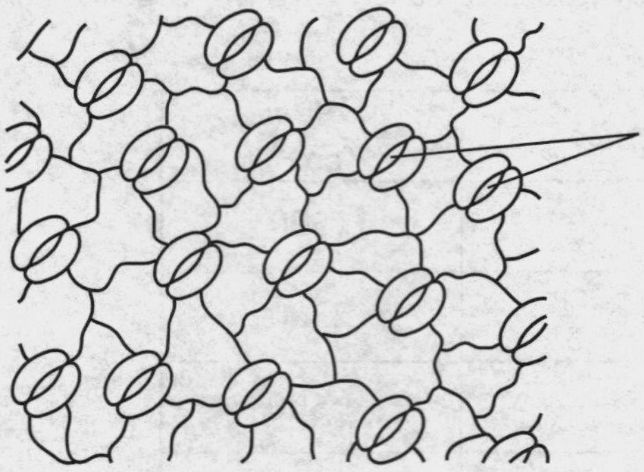

(*a*) (i) Name the pores labelled **X** on the diagram.

____________________________ **1**

(ii) Which gas, needed for photosynthesis, is taken in through these pores?

____________________________ **1**

(iii) The pores are able to open and close. Which substance, important for the growth of the plant, is conserved when the pores are closed?

____________________________ **1**

(*b*) During photosynthesis green plants produce glucose. This can be changed to an insoluble carbohydrate for storage. What is the name of this storage carbohydrate?

____________________________ **1**

(*c*) Name the green substance needed for photosynthesis.

____________________________ **1**

Marks | KU | PS

7. The diagrams show some asexual methods of plant reproduction.

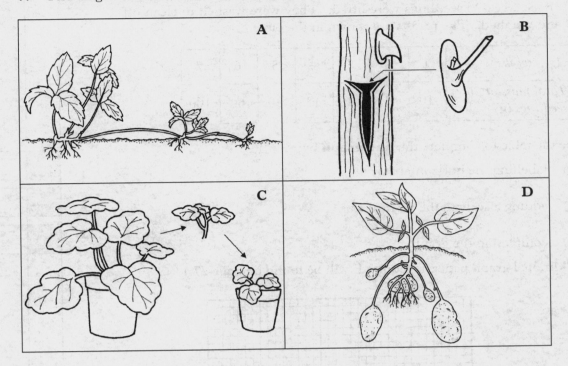

(a) Use the letters of the diagrams to identify the following.

  (i) **Two** artificial methods of reproduction

   letter _____ and _____

  (ii) The diagram that shows reproduction by runners

   letter _____

(b) Name the methods of reproduction shown by diagrams **B** and **D**.

  B _____

  D _____

1

1

1

[Turn over

8. Sweet pea seeds were planted in suitable conditions for germination and growth. Each week 20 seedlings were lifted. They were washed to clean off any soil and weighed. The results are shown in the table.

Age (weeks)	1	2	3	4	5	6	7
Total mass of 20 seedlings (g)	10	7	4	12	30	60	100

(a) Use the table to complete the **line graph** by:

    (i) labelling the horizontal axis   **1**

    (ii) adding a scale to the vertical axis   **1**

    (iii) completing the graph   **1**

(Additional graph paper, if required, will be found on page 27.)

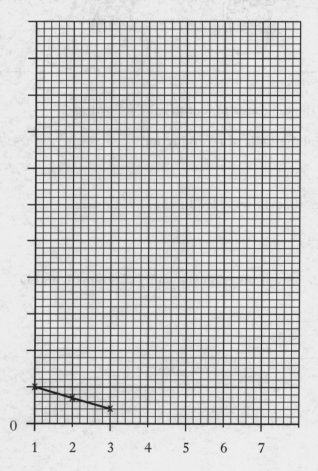

Total mass of 20 seedlings (g)

(b) (i) At what age did the seedlings have the lowest mass?

    _____ weeks   **1**

8. **(b)** **(continued)**

(ii) Between which two weeks was there the greatest increase in mass?
Tick the correct box.

☐ 2 – 3

☐ 3 – 4

☐ 5 – 6

☐ 6 – 7

1

(iii) Calculate the average mass of a single seedling at age seven weeks.
Space for calculation

_____ g

1

(c) (i) Name **two** factors that should be kept the same for all the seedlings during the investigation.

1 _____

2 _____

2

(ii) Weighing 20 seedlings each time reduced the error in weighing single small plants. Suggest **one** other reason for weighing 20 seedlings and calculating an average.

_____

_____

1

(iii) Removing soil from the seedlings reduced a source of error. Suggest **one** further step that should be taken before weighing the seedlings.

_____

1

(d) Predict what difference there would be in the results if the investigation was repeated in the dark.

_____

_____

1

9. The diagram shows some of the structures found in a typical plant cell.

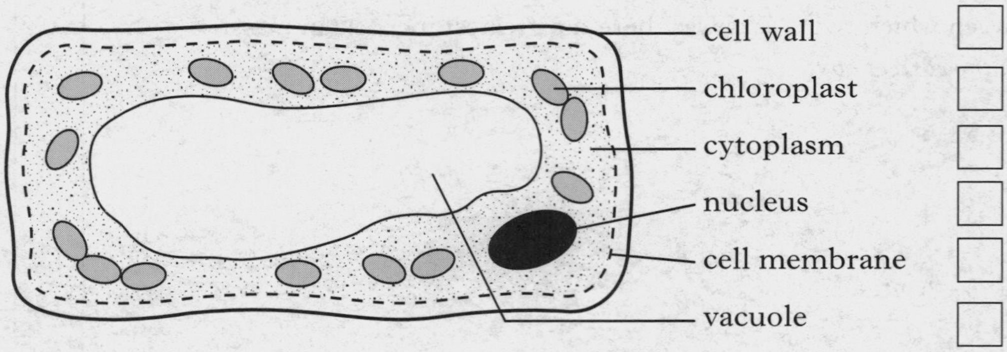

cell wall ☐

chloroplast ☐

cytoplasm ☐

nucleus ☐

cell membrane ☐

vacuole ☐

(a) Tick the boxes to show the structures that are also found in a typical animal cell.

2

(b) Why are cells often stained before being viewed under a microscope?

_____

1

(c) The diagram shows some plant cells as they appear when viewed under a microscope.

field of view = 600 micrometres

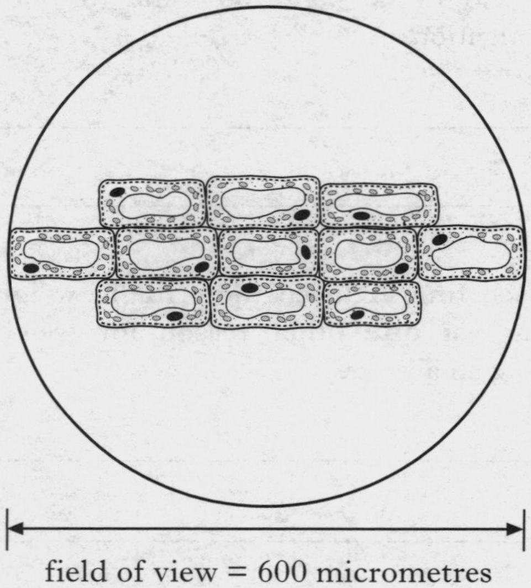

Calculate the average length of the cells.
Space for calculation

_____ micrometres

1

10. The diagram represents aerobic respiration in a cell.

(*a*) Name the substances **W**, **X** and **Y**.

W _____

X _____

Y _____   2

(*b*) What is the source of the substance which is used in respiration and which leads to the formation of carbon dioxide?

_____   1

(*c*) The energy released during respiration can be used for chemical reactions.

Give **two** other ways in which a cell may use this energy.

1 _____

2 _____   1

[Turn over

Marks | KU | PS

11. The apparatus below was used to demonstrate diffusion.

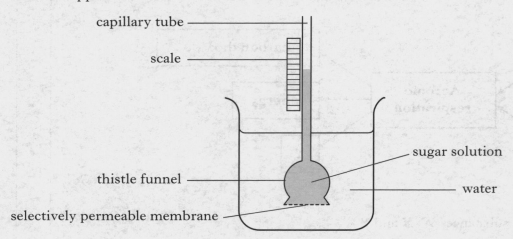

capillary tube

scale

sugar solution

thistle funnel

water

selectively permeable membrane

The height of the sugar solution in the capillary tube was measured at regular intervals. The results are shown in the graph.

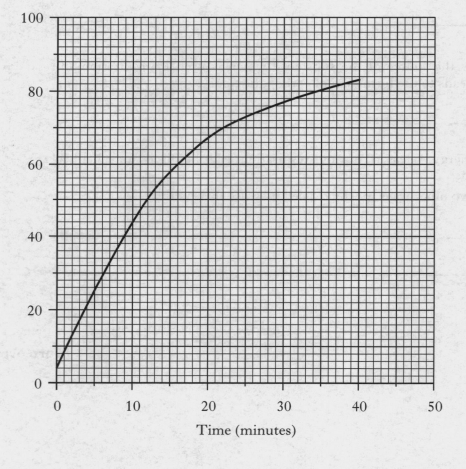

Height of sugar solution (mm)

Time (minutes)

(a) (i) What was the height of the sugar solution in the capillary tube after 10 minutes?

_____ mm

1

11. (a) (continued)

(ii) How long did it take for the sugar solution to rise from 60 mm to 70 mm?

_____ minutes

1

(b) What caused the change in height of the sugar solution in the capillary tube?

Tick the correct box.

Sugar molecules moved out of the funnel. ☐

Sugar molecules moved into the funnel. ☐

Water molecules moved out of the funnel. ☐

Water molecules moved into the funnel. ☐

1

(c) Predict the height of the sugar solution in the capillary tube after 50 minutes.

_____ mm

1

[Turn over

DO NOT
WRITE IN
THIS
MARGIN

Marks | KU | PS

12. Read the passage below.

Adapted from *Dairy Microbiology* by the National Dairy Council.

Yoghurt is a fermented milk product that originated in the Middle East. In that part of the world it tends to be more acidic and thinner than the yoghurt that has been developed in Britain.

Yoghurt can be made from whole milk, skimmed milk, evaporated milk or dried milk. Usually a mixture of these is blended together. The milk used for yoghurt manufacture must be free of all traces of antibiotics. This is to ensure successful fermentation. The blended milk is heated to between 85 °C and 95 °C before being cooled to 32 °C. A starter culture containing bacteria is added and fermentation begins. After 12 hours, the lactic acid content reaches the desired level of between 0·8% and 1·8%.

The yoghurt is now stirred and then fruit may be added before the finished product is packaged and stored at 5 °C. The slower bacterial growth at this temperature gives the yoghurt a shelf life of approximately 10 days. After this time bacterial growth, although restricted, will increase the level of acidity to such an extent as to change the flavour and make it unacceptable to most people.

Answer the questions based on the passage.

(a) Give **two** differences between Middle Eastern yoghurt and British yoghurt.

1 _____

2 _____   1

(b) Other than whole milk, name **two** types of milk used for yoghurt manufacture.

1 _____   2 _____   1

(c) Explain why antibiotics in the milk could prevent successful fermentation.

_____   1

(d) Name the acid produced during yoghurt production.

_____   1

DO NOT WRITE IN THIS MARGIN

	Marks	KU	PS
12. (continued)			
(*e*) What stage in yoghurt production ensures that no unwanted bacteria are present?	1		
(*f*) How does storage at 5 °C increase the shelf life of the yoghurt?	1		
(*g*) What causes the flavour of the yoghurt to change after 10 days storage?	1		

[Turn over

Marks | KU | PS

13. The diagram below shows inheritance of body colour in angelfish.

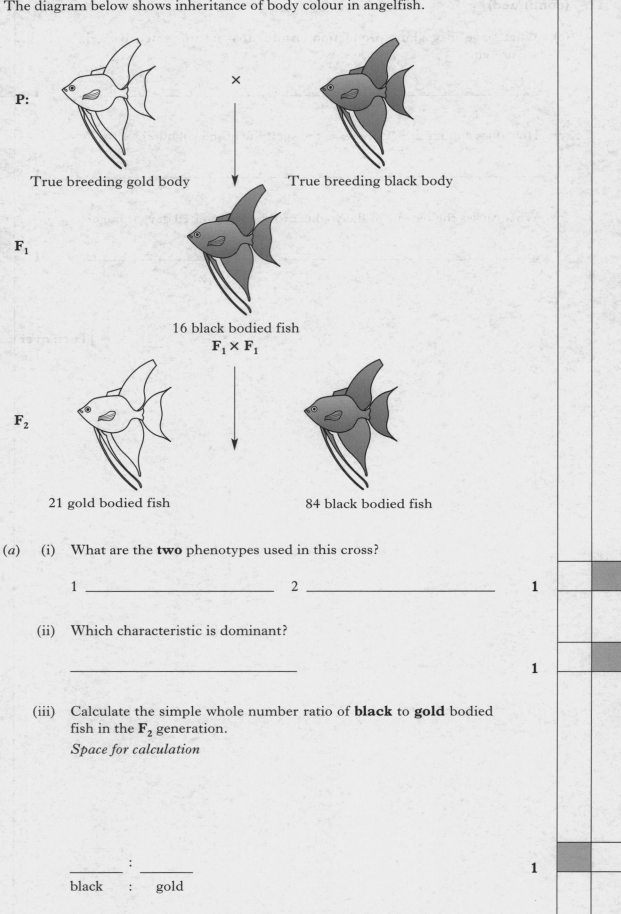

P:

True breeding gold body   True breeding black body

F$_1$

16 black bodied fish
F$_1$ × F$_1$

F$_2$

21 gold bodied fish   84 black bodied fish

(a) (i) What are the **two** phenotypes used in this cross?

1 _____   2 _____   **1**

(ii) Which characteristic is dominant?

_____   **1**

(iii) Calculate the simple whole number ratio of **black** to **gold** bodied fish in the **F$_2$** generation.
Space for calculation

_____ : _____   **1**
black : gold

Marks | KU | PS

13. **(continued)**

(b) Which **one** of the following statements is true?
Tick the correct box.

The parents have the same genotypes and phenotype. ☐

All the F_1 generation have the same genotypes and phenotype. ☐

All the F_2 generation have the same genotypes and phenotype. ☐

1

(c) What type of variation is shown by the body colour of the angelfish?

_____

1

(d) Angelfish produce eggs and sperm for reproduction.
What general name is used for these sex cells?

_____

1

[Turn over

14. The skeleton provides protection for the soft organs of the body.

(a) Give **one** other function of the skeleton.

_____ 1

(b) The diagram shows the structure of a finger joint.

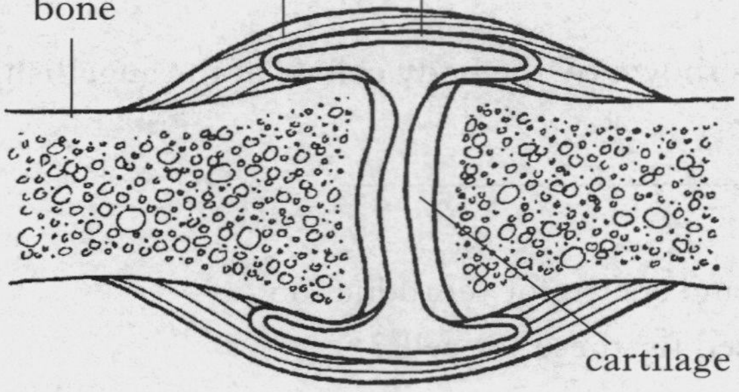

(i) Name the part labelled **A**.

_____ 1

(ii) What is the function of the cartilage in a joint?

_____ 1

(c) Complete the table below about two types of moveable joints.

Range of movement allowed by the joint	Type of joint	Example
One plane		
Many planes		

2

15. The diagram shows apparatus that a pupil used to investigate gas exchange. Air that was breathed in passed through tube A. Air that was breathed out passed through tube B.

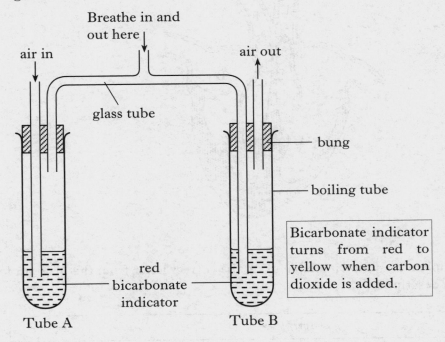

Breathe in and out here

air in

air out

glass tube

bung

boiling tube

Bicarbonate indicator turns from red to yellow when carbon dioxide is added.

red bicarbonate indicator

Tube A   Tube B

(a)   (i)   In which tube would the indicator change colour?

Tube _____

1

(ii)   The other tube acts as a control.
       What is the purpose of a control in an experiment?

       _____

       _____

1

(b)   The experiment was repeated several times using the same apparatus.
       Name **two** variables that would have to be kept constant to make sure the results were valid.

       1 _____

       2 _____

2

[Turn over

Marks | KU | PS

16. The diagram shows the chambers and blood vessels in a heart.

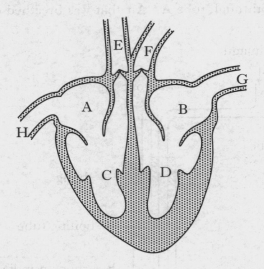

(a) Complete the following table using the correct letter from the diagram for each description.

Description	Letter
The chamber that receives blood from the body.	
The artery that carries blood from the heart to the body.	
The chamber that pumps blood to the lungs.	
The vein that carries blood from the lungs to the heart.	

3

(b) The following sentences are about blood.
Underline **one** option in each bracket to make the sentences correct.

Oxygen is carried in the blood by { red blood cells / white blood cells / plasma }.

Digested food products such as glucose are carried by { red blood cells / white blood cells / plasma }.

2

DO NOT WRITE IN THIS MARGIN

Marks KU PS

17. The following diagram describes some of the stages involved in transferring a gene from a **human chromosome** into a bacterial cell.

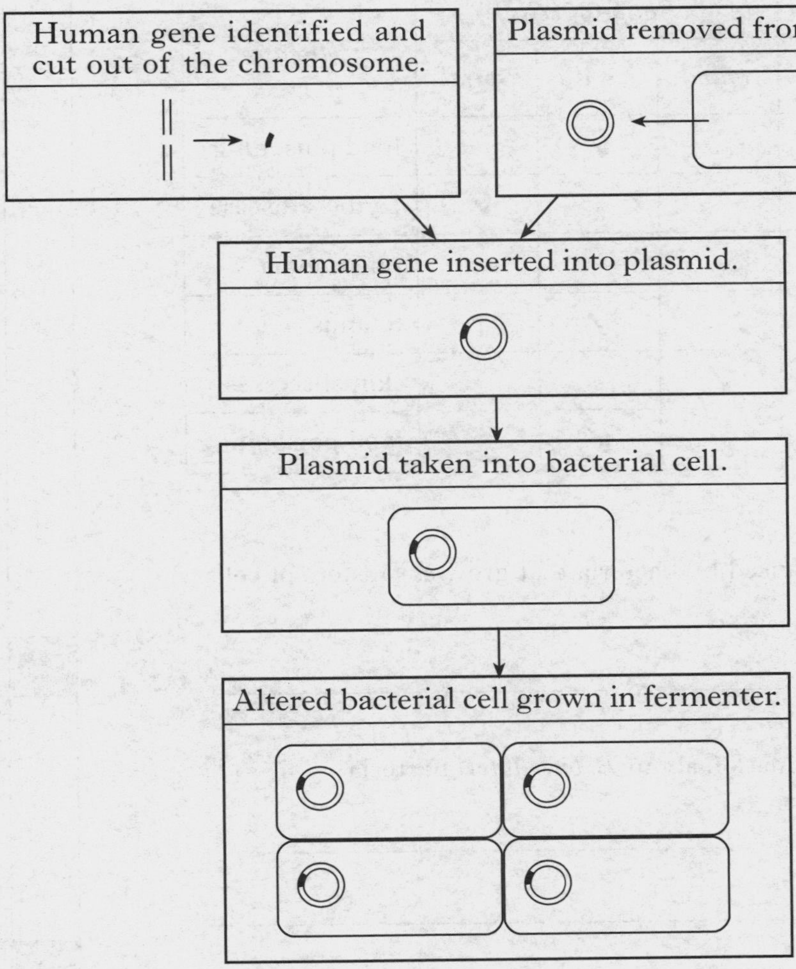

Human gene identified and cut out of the chromosome.
Plasmid removed from bacterial cell.
Human gene inserted into plasmid.
Plasmid taken into bacterial cell.
Altered bacterial cell grown in fermenter.

(*a*) What name is given to this procedure?

______________________________ **1**

(*b*) Give an example of a product that can be made by bacteria as a result of this procedure. State the use of this product.

Product ____________________ **1**

Use ____

____ **1**

(*c*) What type of reproduction is involved during the growth of the bacteria in the fermenter?

________________________ **1**

[Turn over

18. The table gives information about some disease causing bacteria.

Name of bacteria	Pattern of growth		Shape of cells			Disease
	single cells	clusters of cells	round	rod	spiral	
B. cereus		✓		✓		food poisoning
B. burgdoferi	✓				✓	Lyme's disease
S. pneumonia		✓	✓			pneumonia
C. tetani	✓			✓		tetanus
S. aureus		✓	✓			skin abscesses
E. coli	✓			✓		food poisoning

(a) Which **two** diseases are caused by bacteria that grow as clusters of cells and are round in shape?

1 _____ 2 _____   **1**

(b) Give **three** pieces of information about B. burgdoferi bacteria.

1 _____

2 _____

3 _____   **1**

(c) A food sample caused food poisoning.
It was found to contain rod shaped bacteria that grew as single cells.
Name the bacteria.

_____   **1**

[END OF QUESTION PAPER]

SPACE FOR ANSWERS
AND FOR ROUGH WORKING

ADDITIONAL GRID FOR QUESTION 5(*d*)

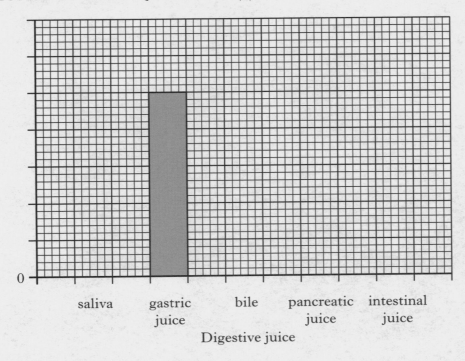

ADDITIONAL GRID FOR QUESTION 8(*a*)

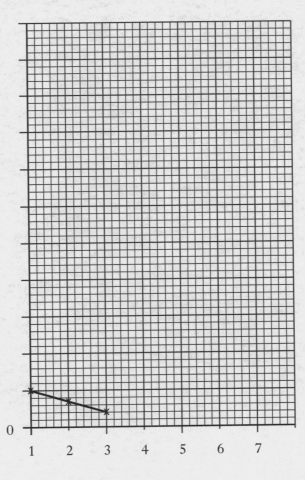

SPACE FOR ANSWERS
AND FOR ROUGH WORKING

2004 | General

[BLANK PAGE]

G

FOR OFFICIAL USE

KU	PS

Total Marks

0300/401

NATIONAL
QUALIFICATIONS
2004

WEDNESDAY, 19 MAY
9.00 AM – 10.30 AM

BIOLOGY
STANDARD GRADE
General Level

Fill in these boxes and read what is printed below.

Full name of centre

Town

Forename(s)

Surname

Date of birth
Day Month Year

Scottish candidate number

Number of seat

1 All questions should be attempted.

2 The questions may be answered in any order but all answers are to be written in the spaces provided in this answer book, and must be written clearly and legibly in ink.

3 Rough work, if any should be necessary, as well as the fair copy, is to be written in this book. Additional spaces for answers and for rough work will be found at the end of the book. Rough work should be scored through when the fair copy has been written.

4 Before leaving the examination room you must give this book to the invigilator. If you do not, you may lose all the marks for this paper.

SCOTTISH
QUALIFICATIONS
AUTHORITY

1. (*a*) The diagram below shows a food web from a woodland ecosystem.

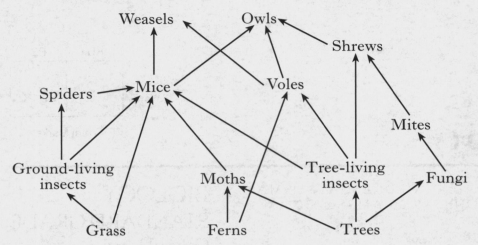

(i) Complete the table below to show each consumer from the food web and its diet.

Consumer	Diet
Mice	spiders, ground-living insects, grass, moths, tree-living insects
Moths	
	grass
Voles	
Weasels	mice, voles
Tree-living insects	trees
	tree-living insects, mites
Fungi	trees
Mites	
	ground-living insects
Owls	

3

1. **(a)** **(continued)**

(ii) Use the food web to complete the food chain below, consisting of four organisms.

| ferns | → | | → | | → | |

1

(b) Trees are producers and mice are consumers.

What is the meaning of the terms producer and consumer?

Producer _____

_____

1

Consumer _____

_____

1

[Turn over

2. Some features of six species of the buttercup family are shown in the table below.

Species name	Leaves	Runners	Stem
Greater spearwort	toothed	present	hairy
Meadow buttercup	lobed	absent	hairy
Lesser celandine	heart-shaped	absent	hairless
Creeping buttercup	lobed	present	hairy
Lesser spearwort	toothed	absent	hairless
Celery-leaved buttercup	lobed	absent	hairless

(a) Use the information in the table to complete the key below.

Write the correct feature on each dotted line and the correct names in the empty boxes.

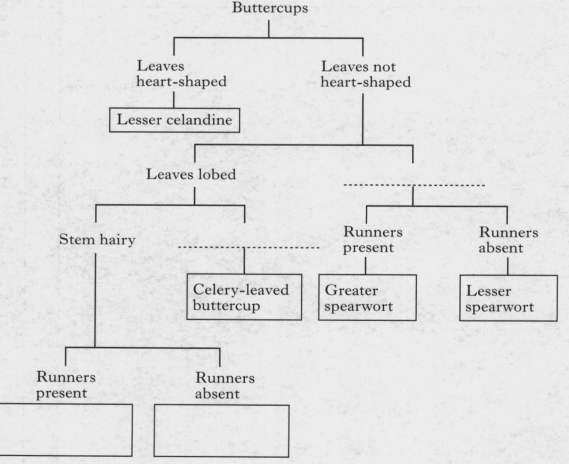

3

Marks | KU | PS

2. **(continued)**

(*b*) Which feature could be used to distinguish between a Lesser celandine and a Lesser spearwort?

_____

1

(*c*) Which features do the Meadow buttercup and the Celery-leaved buttercup have in common?

_____

1

[Turn over

Marks

3. (*a*) A population survey of barnacles and mussels between the high and low tide marks of a rocky shore was carried out using quadrats.

The results are shown in the table below.

Tide mark	High								⟶ Low	
Quadrat number	1	2	3	4	5	6	7	8	9	10
Number of mussels	0	2	15	31	32	34	50	55	58	60
Number of barnacles	52	51	37	40	40	23	15	17	15	10

(i) On the grid below, complete the bar chart by

1. adding a scale to the vertical axis   **1**

2. plotting the bars for the barnacles in quadrats 5–10   **1**

(An additional grid, if needed, will be found on page 27.)

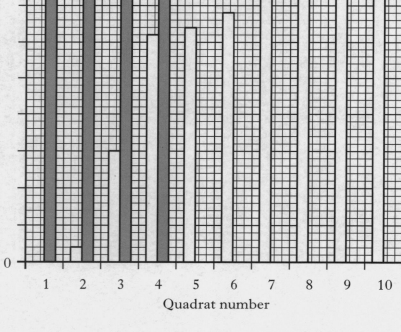

Number of organisms

Quadrat number

□ mussels
■ barnacles

3. **(a)** **(continued)**

(ii) Calculate the average number of barnacles per quadrat.

Space for calculation

Average number _____

1

(iii) What is the trend shown by the number of mussels from the high to the low tide marks?

_____

1

(b) The mussels and the barnacles are in competition with each other.

State **one** possible effect on the mussel population of **reduced competition** from barnacles.

_____

_____

1

(c) The following factors affect populations of barnacles and mussels.

Underline **two** abiotic factors from the list.

List of factors   water temperature

disease

predators

salt concentration

food supply

1

(d) A rocky shore ecosystem consists of a community of organisms and one other part.

Name the other part.

_____

1

[Turn over

4. (*a*) In an investigation on photosynthesis, two bell jars were set up as shown below and left in bright light.

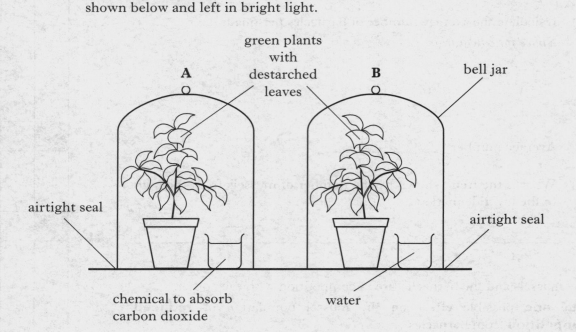

After 48 hours a leaf was removed from each plant and tested for starch.

(i) In which plant would photosynthesis take place? Give a reason for your answer.

Plant _____

Reason _____

_____ **1**

(ii) Name a product of photosynthesis, other than carbohydrate.

_____ **1**

(iii) Why were the plants destarched before being used in the investigation?

_____

_____ **1**

(iv) Give **one** feature of the plants that would have to be kept the same to allow a fair comparison in the investigation.

_____ **1**

4. (continued)

(b) Name the structures in a leaf through which gases can pass.

_____

1

(c) Name the chemical found in leaves that converts light energy into chemical energy during photosynthesis.

_____

1

(d) The grid below refers to parts of a flower.

A sepal	B petal	C stamen	D anther
E stigma	F ovary	G nectary	H ovule

Use letters from the grid to answer the following questions.

(i) Which structure protects the flower bud?

_____

1

(ii) Which structure receives pollen grains?

_____

1

(iii) Which structure develops into a fruit after fertilisation?

_____

1

[Turn over

5. (*a*) The diagram represents the reproductive system of a human female.

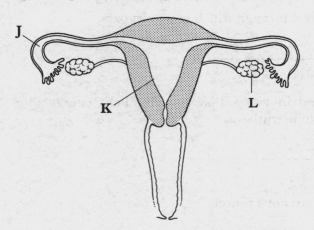

J

K

L

(i) Name the parts labelled on the diagram.

J _____

K _____

L _____

2

(ii) In the table below, match each letter from the diagram to its correct function.

Function	Letter
Eggs produced	
Fertilisation takes place	
Fertilised egg becomes attached	

2

(*b*) Tick (✓) boxes in the table to indicate whether each of the following statements is true for eggs, sperm, or both.

Statement	Eggs	Sperm
Contain a food store for developing fetus		
Swim using a tail		
Produced in testes		
In most fish, are deposited into the water		
Are gametes		

2

6. The apparatus shown was set up to investigate the behaviour of woodlice.

gauze platform   woodlice

Side A   Side B

drying agent   water

At the start of the investigation 20 woodlice were placed in the centre of the chamber. After 10 minutes there were 2 on side A and 18 on side B.

(a) What environmental factor was being investigated?

_____   1

(b) Describe the response of the woodlice in the investigation.

_____

_____   1

(c) Why were the woodlice left for ten minutes before the results were taken?

_____

_____   1

(d) Why were 20 woodlice used, rather than one?

_____   1

(e) Name **one** abiotic factor which should be kept constant during the investigation.

_____   1

(f) Suggest **two** changes which could be made to the apparatus in order to investigate the response of woodlice to light.

1 _____

_____   1

2 _____

_____   1

7. (*a*) Complete the table by using all the letters from the list to identify the parts found in each type of cell.

Each part may be used **once** or **more than once**.

Parts of cells

A   cell membrane
B   cell wall
C   chloroplast
D   cytoplasm
E   nucleus

Leaf cell	Cheek cell

2

(*b*) Use the information in the table below to answer the questions about liquids used in preparing microscope slides.

Type of cell	Liquid used	Effect
human cheek cell	methylene blue	nucleus turns blue
onion epidermal cell	iodine solution	nucleus turns yellow
human skin cell	eosin	cytoplasm turns pink
onion root cell	acetic orcein	chromosomes turn red

(i)   Name **two** liquids used to prepare plant cells.

1 _____

2 _____   1

(ii)   What effect does eosin have on skin cells?

_____   1

(iii) Which liquid could be used to show stages of mitosis?

_____   1

Marks | KU | PS

7. (continued)

(*c*) What name is given to a liquid that is used to make the parts of a cell clearer when viewed under a microscope?

_____

1

(*d*) The magnification of a microscope is calculated using the following formula.

Total magnification = eyepiece lens × objective lens
magnification   magnification

Use the formula to complete the following table.

The same eyepiece was used each time.

Power	Eyepiece lens magnification	Objective lens magnification	Total magnification
Low	× 12	× 4	
Medium		× 10	
High	× 12		× 480

2

[Turn over

Marks | KU | PS

8. (*a*) The statements in the table describe the movement of substances into or out of cells.

Number	Statement
1	glucose moves from the small intestine into the blood
2	water enters root cells from the soil
3	carbon dioxide passes from the blood into the lungs

(i) Which statement is an example of osmosis?

Statement number _____

1

(ii) What term could be used to describe the movement of substances in all of the examples?

_____

1

(*b*) Pieces of potato were weighed, placed in sugar solutions of different concentrations for one hour, then reweighed.

The graph below shows the percentage change in mass at each concentration.

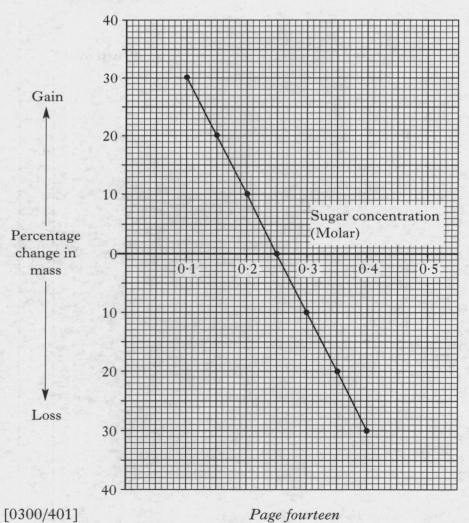

DO NOT
WRITE IN
THIS
MARGIN

Marks | KU | PS

8. **(b)** **(continued)**

(i) The movement of what substance is responsible for the change in mass?

_____

1

(ii) What was the percentage change in mass of the piece of potato placed in the 0·15 Molar solution?

_____ %

1

(iii) What was the concentration of the solution which caused the potato to lose 30% of its original mass?

_____ Molar

1

(iv) At what concentration was there no change in mass of the potato?

_____ Molar

1

[Turn over

DO NOT WRITE IN THIS MARGIN

Marks | KU | PS

9. Read the following passage carefully.

Adapted from "*Stirring Stuff's in the bag*", The Herald, April 2002.

Pausing for a cup of tea is a good way to take time out in a busy day. About 135 million cups are consumed in Britain daily.

Favourite "cuppas" include first thing in the morning before getting ready for work, during a busy day and at the end of the day to relax. Relaxation is the most common mood when taking a tea break.

As well as relieving stress, tea can also be a life-saver. Research has shown that the great British "cuppa" has disease-fighting capabilities. A cup of tea can have protective effects against cancer and heart disease. A mixture of green tea and black tea rubbed on cancerous areas reduced cell growth. Tests show that tea slows the development of lung cancers and some bowel cancers. It is also thought to decrease the risk of cancer of the digestive system. Red tea from South Africa is rich in antioxidants and free from tannin and caffeine which are found in many other teas.

The three basic types of tea, black, green and oolong, give rise to more than 3000 varieties, each having its own distinct character. People are now trying different styles of teas such as organic, Chai spice, decaffeinated, herbal and iced tea.

Answer the following questions, based on the above passage.

(*a*) How much tea is drunk in Britain daily?

_____

1

(*b*) What is the most common mood whilst drinking tea?

_____

1

(*c*) Apart from cancer, what disease can tea help prevent?

_____

1

(*d*) Name **three** types of cancer that tea may help prevent.

1 _____ 2 _____ 3 _____

1

(*e*) What **two** substances are not present in South African red tea?

_____

1

(*f*) Name **three** styles of tea, mentioned in the passage, that people are now trying.

1 _____ 2 _____ 3 _____

1

10. The bar graph shows the body lengths in a population of 300 budgerigars.
The pie chart shows the colours in the same population.

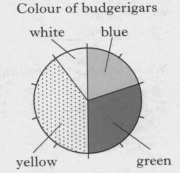

Colour of budgerigars

(a) How many budgerigars are in the range 110 to 119 mm long?
Space for calculation

1

(b) Which of the two characteristics is an example of discontinuous variation?

1

(c) What percentage of the budgerigars are blue?
Space for calculation

_____ %

1

[Turn over

Marks | KU | PS

11. (*a*) An investigation was carried out into the growth of a bacterial culture. The numbers of bacteria were counted every 30 minutes and the results are shown in the table below.

Time (*minutes*)	0	30	60	90	120	150
Number of bacteria (*thousands per mm^3*)	3	6	12	24	48	96

(i) What happens to the number of bacteria every 30 minutes?

_____ 1

(ii) Complete the line graph below by

1   adding a suitable scale to the y-axis   1

2   adding a label to the x-axis   1

3   plotting the graph.   1

(An additional grid, if needed, will be found on page 28.)

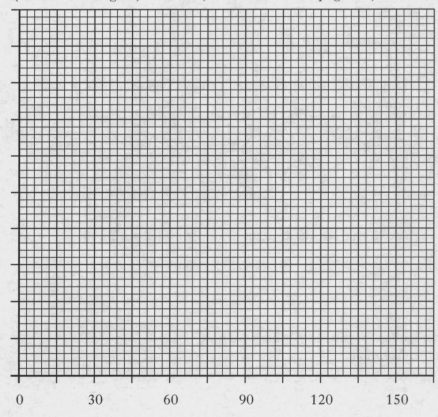

Number of bacteria (thousands per mm^3)

0   30   60   90   120   150

(iii) Assuming no change in conditions, how many bacteria cells would be present after 240 minutes?
Space for calculation

_____ thousands per mm^3 1

Marks | KU | PS

11. **(continued)**

(b) The following diagrams show four stages of mitotic cell division but not in the correct order.

    A   B   C   D

Arrange the letters from the diagrams to put the stages into the correct order. The first stage has been given.

1st stage   C

2nd stage

3rd stage

4th stage   1

(c) Complete the following sentence by underlining the correct option in each group.

In comparison with the original cell, the number of chromosomes present in a cell produced by mitosis is { greater / smaller / the same } and it contains { different / the same } information.

         1

[Turn over

12. (*a*) The diagram shows some of the structures of the human eye.

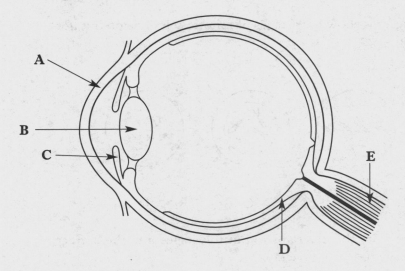

Complete the table to show the names and functions of the structures labelled.

Letter	Name of structure	Function
A		Allows light to enter the eye
B		
C	Iris	
D		Converts light into electrical impulses
E	Optic nerve	

3

(*b*) Humans have two eyes and two ears. What does this contribute to their sight and hearing?

Sight _____

1

_____

Hearing _____

1

_____

Marks KU PS

12. **(continued)**

(*c*) The diagram represents the flow of information in the human nervous system.

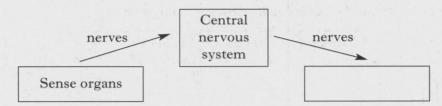

(i) Complete the diagram by writing the missing word in the box. **1**

(ii) Name the two main parts of the central nervous system.

1 _____ 2 _____ **1**

[Turn over

Marks | KU | PS

13. (*a*) The table gives information about components of the blood.
Use the information provided to answer the questions which follow.

Appearance under a microscope (not drawn to the same scale)	Number per mm^3 of blood	Diameter in millimetres	Additional information
Red blood cells	5·5 million	0·008	Made in marrow of bones. Iron essential. 2 million made each second. Last for about 4 months.
White blood cells	8000	0·02	Made in marrow of bones or in lymph nodes. Fight infection by engulfing bacteria or producing antibodies.
Platelets	400,000	0·003	Made in marrow. Contain proteins which form blood clots.

(i) Name **two** places where blood cells are made.

1 _____ 2 _____

1

(ii) Which cells are the largest?

_____

1

(iii) Which component is present in the greatest numbers?

_____

1

(iv) What type of substance is needed to form blood clots?

_____

1

13. (a) (continued)

(v) Describe **two** ways in which white blood cells fight infection.

1 _____

2 _____

1

(vi) On average, how many red blood cells are made in an hour?
Space for calculation

_____ million

1

(b) The diagram below represents the site of gas exchange between a blood vessel and the muscle cells of a mammal.

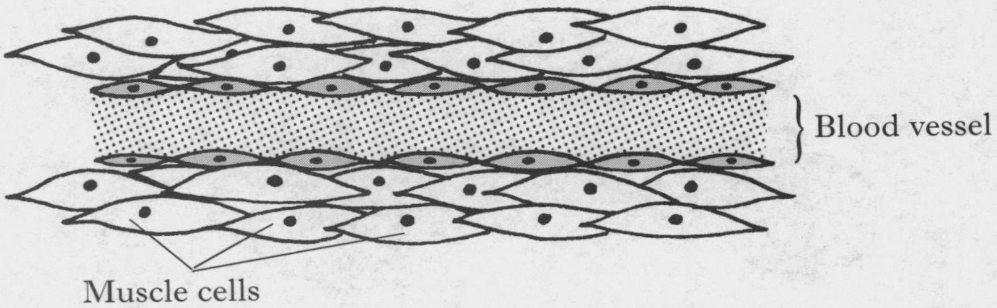

Muscle cells

Blood vessel

(i) Name the type of blood vessel shown.

_____

1

(ii) On the diagram, write the letter **H** to indicate an area where the oxygen concentration is relatively high and the letter **L** to indicate where it is relatively low.

1

(c) In which component of blood is most of the oxygen carried?

_____

1

[Turn over

Marks | KU | PS

14. (a) A mule is produced by mating a horse and a donkey.
Mules are always infertile. What information does this provide about horses and donkeys?

_____ 1

(b) The diagram below shows inheritance of colour in onions.

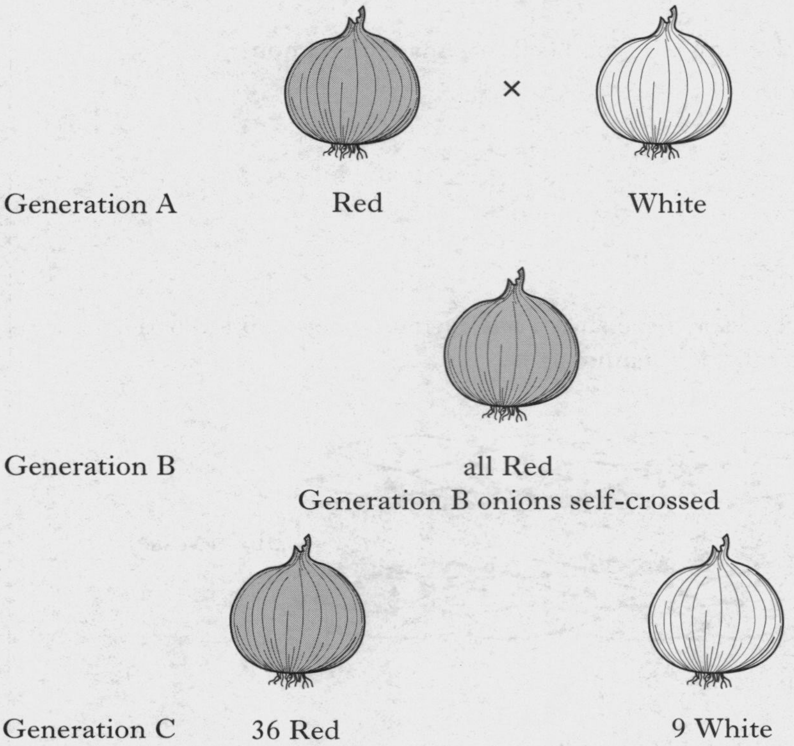

Generation A   Red   ×   White

Generation B   all Red
Generation B onions self-crossed

Generation C   36 Red   9 White

(i) Which onion colour is dominant?

_____ 1

(ii) Complete the table with the correct symbols to identify each of the generations shown in the diagram.

Generation	Symbol
A	**P**
B	
C	

1

(iii) Calculate the simple whole number ratio of red onions to white onions produced in Generation C.

Space for calculation

_____ : _____
Red onions   White onions   1

15. Thalassaemia is an inherited disease which prevents people producing blood cells. The family tree shows inheritance of thalassaemia.

☐ Unaffected male   ▨ Thalassaemic male

○ Unaffected female   ⬤ Thalassaemic female

(a)   (i)   Which of the following statements about Parents A and B is true?
Tick (✓) the correct box.

Both have the thalassaemic gene.   ☐

One has the thalassaemic gene.   ☐

Neither has the thalassaemic gene.   ☐   **1**

(ii)   Give a reason for your answer.

_____   **1**

(b)   What proportion of the children of Parents A and B were thalassaemic?

_____   **1**

(c)   Doctors can test for thalassaemia by examining the cells of a fetus. The cells are obtained by inserting a needle into the mother's uterus and withdrawing fluid from around the fetus.
What name is given to this procedure?

_____   **1**

[Turn over

Marks | KU | PS

16. Yeast is a micro-organism which carries out fermentation.

(*a*) Complete the following word equation for fermentation in yeast.

	→		+		+	**energy**

1

(*b*) Name **two** manufacturing processes which depend on fermentation by yeast.

1 _____

2 _____

1

(*c*) Complete the following sentence by underlining the correct word in each group.

Yeast is a $\left\{ \begin{array}{c} \text{fungus} \\ \text{bacterium} \end{array} \right\}$ and is $\left\{ \begin{array}{c} \text{single-} \\ \text{multi-} \end{array} \right\}$ celled.

1

(*d*) Describe the precautions which should be taken with each of the following items when working with micro-organisms.

1 Bench surfaces _____

_____

1

2 Wire loops for inoculating a plate _____

_____

1

(*e*) Petri dishes half-filled with agar gel are used to grow micro-organisms.

Explain why Petri dishes containing micro-organisms must be kept closed.

_____

1

[*END OF QUESTION PAPER*]

SPACE FOR ANSWERS
AND FOR ROUGH WORKING

ADDITIONAL GRID FOR QUESTION 3(*a*)(i)

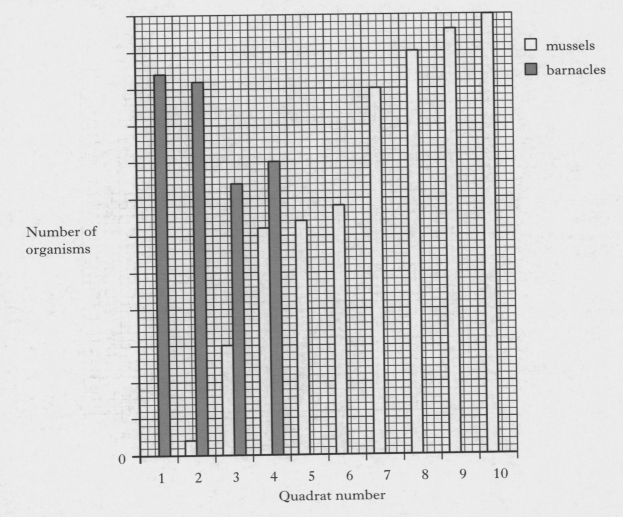

SPACE FOR ANSWERS
AND FOR ROUGH WORKING

ADDITIONAL GRID FOR QUESTION 11(*a*)(ii)

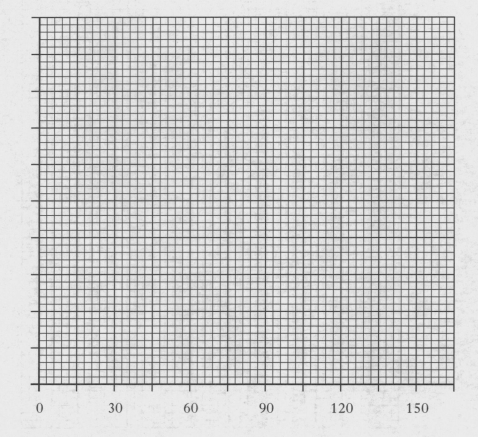

Number of
bacteria
(thousands
per mm^3)

[BLANK PAGE]

FOR OFFICIAL USE

KU	PS

Total Marks

0300/401

NATIONAL
QUALIFICATIONS
2005

WEDNESDAY, 18 MAY
9.00 AM – 10.30 AM

**BIOLOGY
STANDARD GRADE**
General Level

Fill in these boxes and read what is printed below.

Full name of centre

Town

Forename(s)

Surname

Date of birth
Day Month Year

Scottish candidate number

Number of seat

1 All questions should be attempted.

2 The questions may be answered in any order but all answers are to be written in the spaces provided in this answer book, and must be written clearly and legibly in ink.

3 Rough work, if any should be necessary, as well as the fair copy, is to be written in this book. Additional spaces for answers and for rough work will be found at the end of the book. Rough work should be scored through when the fair copy has been written.

4 Before leaving the examination room you must give this book to the invigilator. If you do not, you may lose all the marks for this paper.

SCOTTISH
QUALIFICATIONS
AUTHORITY

1. Part of a woodland food web is shown below.

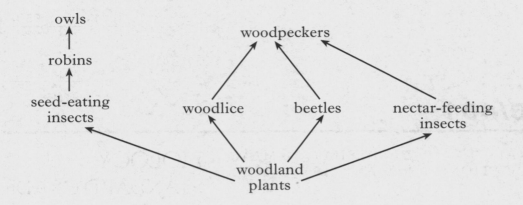

(a) (i) What do the arrows in the food web represent?

_____

1

(ii) How many food chains in the food web involve woodpeckers?

_____

1

(iii) Blue tits eat woodlice. Hawks eat blue tits and robins.

Add blue tits and hawks to the food web diagram to show their feeding relationships.

1

(b) A study of the populations of beetles and woodlice in an area of woodland was carried out over a number of years.

The results are shown below.

Year of study	Number of beetles	Number of woodlice
1	563	540
2	641	672
3	682	698
4	117	940

(i) Use information from **both** the table **and** the food web to suggest an explanation for the drop in the number of beetles in year 4 of the study.

_____

_____

1

1.(b) (continued)

(ii) During the same period, the numbers of owls increased.

Explain this change in terms of their birth rate and death rate.

_____

_____   1

(iii) What change in the population of the robins could have caused the increase in the number of owls?

_____   1

(c) When a plant or animal dies, decay takes place.

Choose words from the box below to complete the following sentences about decay.

You may use each word **once**, **more than once** or **not at all**.

soil	animals	nutrients
plants	protein	micro-organisms

Decay is carried out by _____ .

This process releases _____ which can be absorbed

by _____ .   2

[Turn over

Marks | KU | PS

2. (a) The following table gives the results of an investigation on the factors affecting seed germination.

Test tube	Conditions provided		
	Temperature (°C)	Water present	Oxygen present
1	20	yes	yes
2	20	yes	no
3	20	no	yes
4	0	yes	yes
5	0	no	yes

In which tube(s) would germination occur?

_____

1

(b) The diagram shows a section through a seed.

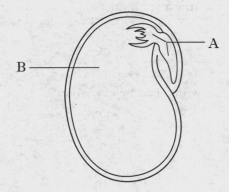

(i) Name the parts labelled A and B.

A _____

1

B _____

1

(ii) Name the part of a seed which protects the internal structures.

_____

1

2. **(continued)**

(c) The table below shows the time from germination to flowering for some plant species.

Plant species	Time from germination to flowering (years)
Rock rose	2·0
Hollyhock	0·5
Broom	3·0
Birch	10·0
Phlox	1·0
Berberis	5·5

Use the information from the table to complete the **bar chart** below by:

(i) labelling the vertical axis;   **1**

(ii) adding an appropriate scale to the vertical axis;   **1**

(iii) drawing the bars.   **1**

(Additional graph paper, if required, will be found on page 30.)

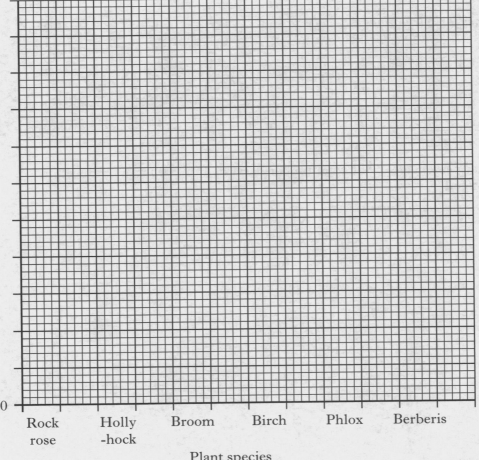

Plant species

[Turn over

Marks

3. The table below gives information about the harvest of softwood timber over a 3 year period.

Country	Timber harvested each year (m³)		
	1999	2000	2001
Scotland	2292	2496	2883
England	699	881	913
Wales	385	463	663
Total		3840	

(a) Complete the table to show the totals harvested in 1999 and in 2001.

Space for calculations

1

(b) What was the increase in timber harvested in Wales between 1999 and 2001?

Space for calculation

_____ m³

1

(c) What percentage of the total timber harvested in 2000 was produced in Scotland?

Space for calculation

_____ %

1

Marks | KU | PS

4. The following sentences refer to food manufacture and transport in plants. Underline **one** alternative in each bracket to make the sentences correct.

(*a*) Light energy is converted to chemical energy by $\left\{ \begin{array}{l} \text{carbon dioxide} \\ \text{chlorophyll} \end{array} \right\}$.

1

(*b*) Food is transported from the leaves in $\left\{ \begin{array}{l} \text{xylem} \\ \text{phloem} \end{array} \right\}$.

1

(*c*) The raw materials for photosynthesis are $\left\{ \begin{array}{l} \text{carbon dioxide} \\ \text{oxygen} \end{array} \right\}$ and

$\left\{ \begin{array}{l} \text{glucose} \\ \text{water} \end{array} \right\}$.

1

(*d*) Food may be stored in the leaves as $\left\{ \begin{array}{l} \text{glucose} \\ \text{starch} \end{array} \right\}$.

1

[Turn over

DO NOT
WRITE IN
THIS
MARGIN

Marks | KU | PS

5. The diagram shows a choice chamber which could be used to investigate the behaviour of woodlice.

woodlice

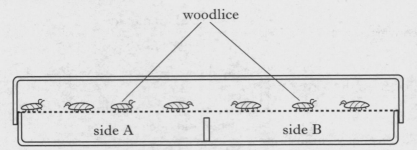

side A   side B

(*a*) How could the choice chamber be set up to study the effect of light on the behaviour of woodlice?

_____

_____

1

(*b*) (i) Name **one** other abiotic factor which may affect woodlice behaviour that can be investigated using a choice chamber.

_____

1

(ii) How could the choice chamber be set up to investigate this other abiotic factor?

_____

_____

1

6. The effect of practice on the reaction times of three volunteers was investigated. A buzzer was sounded and the time taken to stop a clock was measured.

Each volunteer was tested 10 times.

The results are shown in the table.

	Reaction time (milliseconds)									
Attempt / Volunteer	1	2	3	4	5	6	7	8	9	10
A	256	250	210	207	201	192	187	164	162	154
B	234	227	218	201	200	185	179	161	153	147
C	218	200	195	192	186	178	160	149	136	131

(a) Why were three volunteers tested rather than one?

_____

1

(b) The average reaction time of the three volunteers' first attempts was 236 milliseconds.

Calculate the average reaction time of their final attempts.

Space for calculation

_____ milliseconds

1

(c) From the results of the investigation, describe the effect of practice on reaction time.

_____

_____

1

[Turn over

Marks | KU | PS

7. (a) The following list contains descriptions of stages in the reproduction of a mammal.

A   A sperm nucleus joins with an egg nucleus.
B   The embryo develops in the amniotic sac.
C   The embryo becomes attached to the uterus wall.
D   A fertilised egg passes down the oviduct.
E   The young animal is born.

Arrange the stages into the correct order by writing the letters into the boxes.

1

(b) The diagrams show the human female and male reproductive systems.

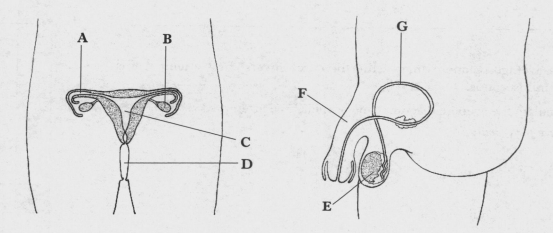

Complete the table below by adding the correct letter, name and function of the parts.

Letter	Name	Function
	ovary	
		where the embryo develops
E		

3

DO NOT WRITE IN THIS MARGIN

Marks | KU | PS

7. (continued)

(*c*) (i) Mammal embryos obtain their food from their mother's blood.

Where do the embryos of fish obtain their food?

______________________________ 1

(ii) Young fish care for themselves.

How are young mammals cared for?

______________________________ 1

[Turn over

Official SQA Past Papers: General Biology 2005

DO NOT
WRITE IN
THIS
MARGIN

Marks | KU | PS

8. (*a*) The diagram represents a section through the heart of a mammal.

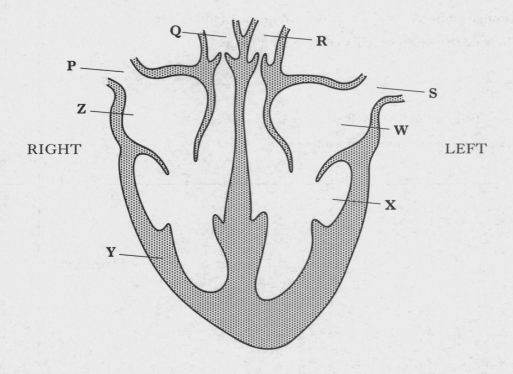

Use letters from the diagram to identify the following.

   (i)   The two atria (auricles).

       _____ and _____

   (ii) The vessel which brings blood to the heart from the lungs.

       _____

   (iii) The two vessels which carry deoxygenated blood.

       _____ and _____

(*b*) Explain why the wall of the left ventricle is thicker than the wall of the right ventricle.

   _____

   _____

1

1

1

1

8. **(continued)**

(*c*) (i) Use lines to connect each of the blood vessels to the correct description of blood flow.

Blood vessel   *Description of blood flow*

| arteries | | away from the heart |

| veins | | through the tissues |

| capillaries | | towards the heart |

2

(ii) In which type of blood vessel may a pulse be felt?

_____

1

[Turn over

Marks | KU | PS

9. The pulse rate of an athlete was monitored during a training exercise.
The results are shown in the table.

Time (minutes)	0	1	2	3	4	5	6	7	8
Pulse rate (beats per minute)	65	65	90	118	118	118	105	100	80

(*a*) Complete the line graph of the results by

   (i) labelling and adding an appropriate scale to the horizontal axis,   **1**

   (ii) plotting the graph.   **1**

The first three points have been plotted.

(Additional graph paper, if required, will be found on page 31.)

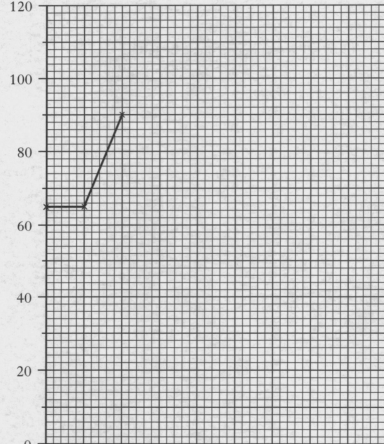

(*b*) What evidence suggests that the athlete had not fully recovered at 8 minutes?

_____

    1

DO NOT WRITE IN THIS MARGIN

Marks | KU | PS

9. (continued)

(*c*) Suggest an improvement to the procedure to allow the recovery time of the athlete to be measured.

____

____ **1**

(*d*) How might the recovery time of the athlete differ from that of an untrained person?

____

____ **1**

[Turn over

Marks | KU | PS

10. Read the following passage and answer the questions based on it.

Hayfever

Hayfever affects 2 to 3 million people in Britain. It is caused by an allergy to pollen or sometimes the spores of fungi. The body's immune system reacts by releasing excess histamine. This results in an irritation and inflammation of the nose and eyes.

The symptoms vary and may involve sneezing, a runny or blocked nose, and a sore throat. The eyes may become red, watery or itchy. In addition, a wheezy chest may suggest that the sufferer also has asthma. The peak pollen time is early summer when school and university examinations take place. This can make it difficult to revise and perform well.

Hayfever is related to asthma and eczema. It is quite common to find members of the same family with one or more of these conditions.

Various treatments are available without prescription. These include antihistamine tablets to reduce the allergic response as well as nasal sprays and eye drops to reduce inflammation. For severe cases, doctors may prescribe either tablets or injections containing steroids. These can cause side effects so the benefits have to be weighed against the possible disadvantages. Tablets are more favoured than injections. Other types of injection can desensitise patients to the pollen causing their allergy. Unfortunately, they may produce serious side effects and, as they can only be given under close hospital supervision, are hardly ever used.

(a) What effect does pollen have on the body's immune system in hayfever sufferers?

_____ 1

(b) What evidence is there that hayfever might have a genetic component?

_____ 1

(c) Which symptom suggests that a hayfever sufferer may also have asthma?

_____ 1

Marks | KU | PS

10. **(continued)**

(d) At what time of the year are hayfever sufferers likely to be worst affected?

_____

1

(e) What type of substance is found in treatments prescribed for severe cases of hayfever?

_____

1

(f) Why are desensitising injections not used very often?

_____

1

[Turn over

Marks | KU | PS

11. (*a*) The bar chart shows the results of a survey into blood groups of a sample of people in a Scottish town (Town X).

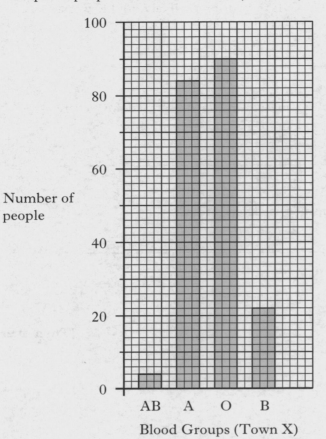

Blood Groups (Town X)

(i) Is the variation in blood group continuous or discontinuous?

_____

1

(ii) How many people were in the survey?
Space for calculation

Number of people _____

1

Marks KU PS

11. (continued)

(*b*) A similar survey was carried out on a sample of 1000 people in a different town of the same size (Town Y).

There were 20 with group AB, 500 with group A, 400 with group O and 80 with group B.

(i) Complete the pie chart of these results by drawing and labelling the remaining segments.

(An additional chart, if required, will be found on page 31.)

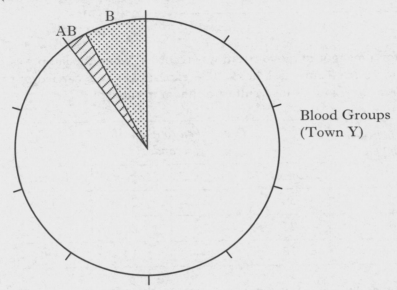

Blood Groups
(Town Y)

2

(ii) What percentage of people in the Town Y sample had blood group O?

Space for calculation

_____ %

1

(*c*) (i) Select **one** similarity and **one** difference between the results of the surveys for Towns X and Y.

Similarity _____

1

Difference _____

1

(ii) Which blood group survey, Town X or Town Y, is the more reliable?

Give a reason for your answer.

Town _____

1

Reason _____

1

12. Maggots move away from light. The effect of different light intensities on the rate of movement was investigated using the apparatus shown below.

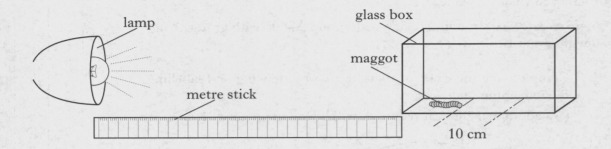

The time taken for a maggot to move 10 cm was recorded when the lamp was at different distances from the glass box. The experiment was carried out using three different maggots. The results are shown in the table.

Distance between lamp and box (cm)	Time taken to move 10 cm (seconds)			
	Maggot 1	Maggot 2	Maggot 3	Average
100	30	33	30	31
50	23	24	22	
25	18	20	19	19

(a) Complete the table with the average time for the maggots to move 10 cm when the lamp was at a distance of 50 cm.

Space for calculation

1

(b) Underline **one** option in each bracket to complete the following sentences correctly.

As the distance between the lamp and the glass box decreases, the light

intensity $\left\{ \begin{array}{l} \text{increases} \\ \text{decreases} \\ \text{stays the same} \end{array} \right\}$.

1

As the light intensity decreases, the time taken for the maggot to move

10 cm $\left\{ \begin{array}{l} \text{increases} \\ \text{decreases} \\ \text{stays the same} \end{array} \right\}$.

1

(c) What would happen to the rate of movement of the maggots if they were placed in darkness?

_____

1

13. Phosphorylase is an enzyme extracted from potatoes. Drops of phosphorylase, glucose-1-phosphate and water were added to a dimple tile as shown.

Row A	phosphorylase + glucose-1-phosphate
Row B	phosphorylase + water
Row C	glucose-1-phosphate + water

A drop of iodine solution was added to one dimple in each row at three-minute intervals. If starch is present, a black colour forms.

The results are shown below.

Time of adding iodine solution

0   3   6   9 minutes

Row A

Row B

Row C

(a) In which row has starch been synthesised?

Row _____

1

(b) The experiment was carried out at 25 °C. How would the results in Row A differ if the experiment had been carried out at a lower temperature?

_____

1

(c) Rows B and C are control experiments.

(i) What conclusion can be drawn from Row B? _____

_____

1

(ii) What conclusion can be drawn from Row C? _____

_____

1

[Turn over

14. The diagrams show two different types of enzyme-controlled reactions.

**Diagram 1
Synthesis reaction**

new product

enzyme
molecule

substrate
molecules

**Diagram 2
Breakdown reaction**

enzyme
molecule

2 new
products
formed

substrate
molecule

(a) For each of the following word equations state whether it is an example of a synthesis reaction or a breakdown reaction.

Word equation   *Type of reaction*

(i) maltose $\xrightarrow{\textbf{enzyme X}}$ glucose molecules _____

(ii) amino acid molecules $\xrightarrow{\textbf{enzyme Y}}$ protein molecule _____

(iii) fatty acids and glycerol $\xrightarrow{\textbf{enzyme Z}}$ fat molecule _____   **2**

(b) Of what type of substance are enzymes made?

_____   **1**

(c) Respiration provides energy for cells to carry out various functions.

Underline **two** of the following functions which require energy from respiration.

Muscle contraction   Osmosis   Diffusion   Cell division   **1**

15. (*a*) The following grid contains some terms used in studying inheritance.

A gamete formation	B tallness in peas	C genotype
D phenotype	E true breeding	F gene
G fertilisation	H dominant	I dwarfness in peas

Use letters from the grid to identify the correct term for each of the following.

(i) Part of a chromosome   ———   1

(ii) Involves a reduction in the number of chromosomes   ———   1

(iii) Two different phenotypes of the same characteristic   ———

and   ———   1

(iv) An organism with only one form of a particular gene   ———   1

(v) The genes that an organism contains for a characteristic   ———   1

(*b*) Pea plant cells contain 14 chromosomes.

(i) How many complete sets of chromosomes does this represent?

_____ sets   1

(ii) How many chromosomes are there in the sex cells of pea plants?
Space for calculation

_____ chromosomes   1

[Turn over

Marks | KU | PS

16. The diagram shows the apparatus used to produce large numbers of bacterial cells for manufacturing insulin.

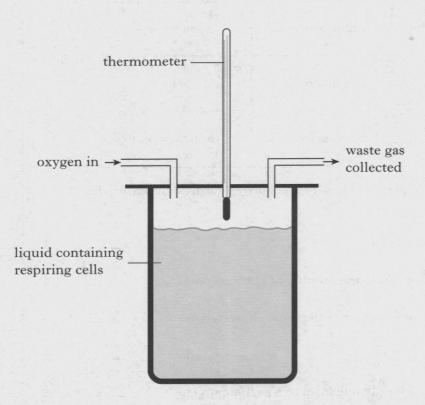

thermometer

oxygen in →

waste gas collected

liquid containing respiring cells

(a) Suggest an improvement which could be made to the way the apparatus is set up and explain why it is necessary.

Improvement _____ 1

Explanation _____

_____ 1

(b) (i) Which type of respiration will take place because of the presence of oxygen?

_____ 1

(ii) What additional factor, not shown in the diagram, must be supplied to allow the bacteria to respire?

_____ 1

Marks | KU | PS

16. **(b)** **(continued)**

(iii) What waste gas will be produced during respiration?

_____ 1

(iv) What form of energy, other than chemical, may be released by the bacterial cells during respiration?

_____ 1

[Turn over

Marks | KU | PS

17. A sewage works removes organic material before water is discharged into a river. This is done in two main stages.

Stage 1   Organic solids settle out as sludge which is treated separately.

Stage 2   The remaining liquid is treated with living organisms.

(a)   (i)   Name **one** useful product which can be made from the treated sludge produced in Stage 1.

_____

1

(ii)   What type of organisms act on the liquid in Stage 2?

_____

1

(iii)   Describe **one** way in which oxygen can be provided for the organisms in Stage 2.

_____

_____

1

17. **(continued)**

(b) When water from a sewage works is analysed, several measurements are made. The table shows some of the measurements taken over one year.

Month	Suspended solids (mg/l)	Biochemical oxygen demand (mg/l)
January	35·0	31·0
February	42·0	40·0
March	44·0	35·5
April	30·5	18·0
May	27·0	17·0
June	29·5	19·0
July	21·5	14·5
August	25·5	16·5
September	25·5	16·5
October	29·5	22·0
November	34·5	28·5
December	32·5	35·0

(i) Sewage works should not discharge water with more than 30 mg/l suspended solids **and** a biochemical oxygen demand of more than 20 mg/l.

In which months of the year was water from the sewage works not meeting this standard?

_____

_____ **1**

(ii) Suggest **one** abiotic factor which affects how well the living organisms break down the sewage over the course of a year.

_____ **1**

[Turn over

18. An investigation was carried out into the effects of various additives on dough. Yeast was mixed with flour and sugar solution to make dough. The dough was then cut into four pieces and additives were added to three of them. 20 cm³ of each dough was put into measuring cylinders and the volume of the dough was measured after one hour.

The results are shown below.

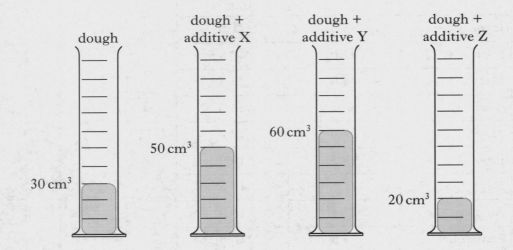

(a) Calculate the percentage increase in the volume of the dough with no additive.

Space for calculation

_____%   1

(b) What substance produced by yeast caused the dough to rise?

_____   1

(c) Which additive caused the greatest increase in the volume of the dough?

_____   1

(d) Which additive may have prevented the yeast fermenting?

_____   1

(e) What type of organism is yeast?

_____   1

Marks | KU | PS

19. (a) Pollution can affect areas such as fresh water and seas.

Name the **two** other main areas which can be affected by pollution.

1 _____

2 _____

1

(b) Complete the table to show the **three** main sources of pollution and **one** example of a pollutant from each.

Source	Example of pollutant
industry	
	fertilisers
	litter

2

(c) Pollution from the exhausts of vehicles can be a major problem in some cities.

Give **one** way in which this type of pollution can be controlled.

_____

_____

1

[END OF QUESTION PAPER]

[Turn over

SPACE FOR ANSWERS
AND FOR ROUGH WORKING

ADDITIONAL GRID FOR QUESTION 2(c)

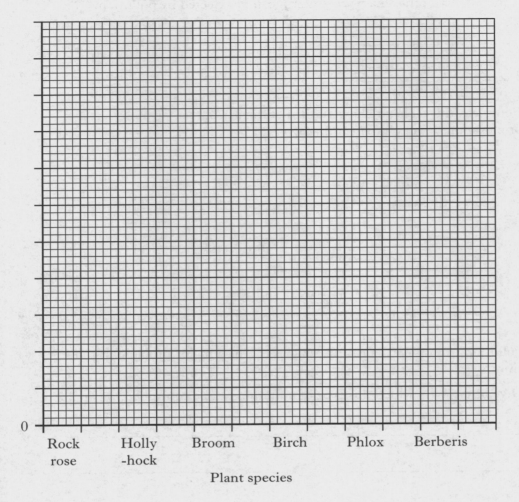

0

Rock
rose

Holly
-hock

Broom

Birch

Phlox

Berberis

Plant species

SPACE FOR ANSWERS
AND FOR ROUGH WORKING

ADDITIONAL GRID FOR QUESTION 9(*a*)

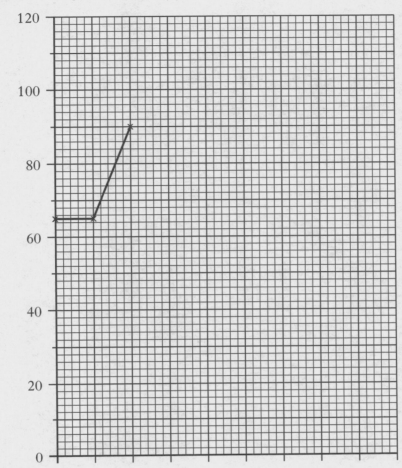

ADDITIONAL GRID FOR QUESTION 11(*b*)(i)

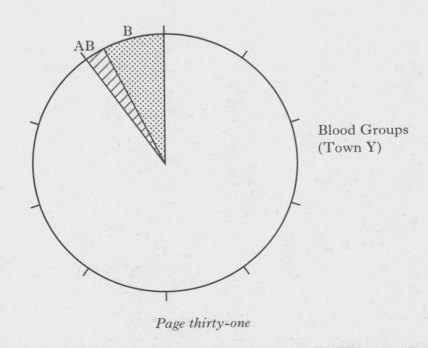

Blood Groups
(Town Y)

SPACE FOR ANSWERS
AND FOR ROUGH WORKING

Page thirty-two

[BLANK PAGE]

FOR OFFICIAL USE

G

KU	PS

Total Marks

0300/401

NATIONAL
QUALIFICATIONS
2006

TUESDAY, 23 MAY
9.00 AM – 10.30 AM

BIOLOGY
STANDARD GRADE
General Level

Fill in these boxes and read what is printed below.

Full name of centre

Town

Forename(s)

Surname

Date of birth

Day   Month   Year   Scottish candidate number   Number of seat

1   All questions should be attempted.

2   The questions may be answered in any order but all answers are to be written in the spaces provided in this answer book, and must be written clearly and legibly in ink.

3   Rough work, if any should be necessary, as well as the fair copy, is to be written in this book. Additional spaces for answers and for rough work will be found at the end of the book. Rough work should be scored through when the fair copy has been written.

4   Before leaving the examination room you must give this book to the invigilator. If you do not, you may lose all the marks for this paper.

SCOTTISH
QUALIFICATIONS
AUTHORITY

1. (a) The grid contains some terms related to the biosphere.

A community	B competition	C ecosystem	D food shortage
E habitat	F light intensity	G population	H predation

Use letters from the grid to complete the following statements.

(i) An ecosystem is made up of ☐ and ☐ .

1

(ii) The interaction between organisms which need the same resources is called ☐ .

1

(iii) An example of an abiotic factor is ☐ .

1

(b) Describe what is meant by the term *a population*.

_____

_____

1

1. (continued)

(c) The table shows the results of an investigation into the distribution of ling heather and bell heather in an area of moorland.

	Quadrat number				
	1	2	3	4	5
Type of heather present	Ling	Bell	Ling and Bell	Bell	Ling
Soil moisture (units from meter)	4	6	5	7	3
Soil pH	5·6	5·5	5·3	5·6	5·4
Soil temperature (°C)	4	7	8	4	7

(i) Calculate the average soil moisture reading in the investigation area.
Space for calculation

_____ units

(ii) The soil pH was measured using a soil pH meter. Describe how the average pH of the soil in a single quadrat is calculated.

_____

_____

(iii) Which abiotic factor appears to have the greatest effect on the distribution of the two types of heather? Give a reason for your answer.

Factor _____

Reason _____

_____

(iv) The quadrat used was a square wooden frame.
Describe how a quadrat should be used to investigate the plants present in an area.

_____

_____

2. An investigation into the effect of soil moisture on the germination of seeds was carried out using the apparatus shown below. Seeds were sown evenly over the whole surface of the soil.

The diagram shows the internal detail of the apparatus.

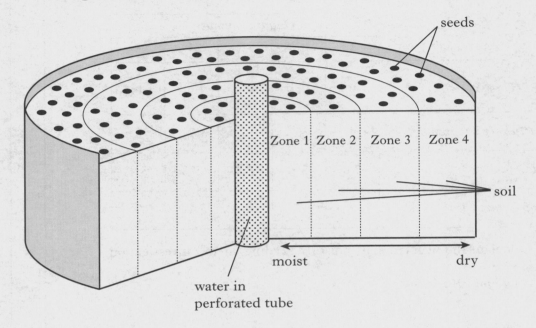

After five days, the percentage of the seeds which had germinated and the average soil moisture in each zone were recorded.

The results are shown in the table.

	Zone 1	Zone 2	Zone 3	Zone 4
Average soil moisture (cm³ per 100 g)	90	70	50	30
Seeds germinated (%)	80	100	72	38

DO NOT
WRITE IN
THIS
MARGIN

Marks KU PS

2. (continued)

(a) Use the results to complete the bar chart of the germination of the seeds by:

   (i) putting the scale on the vertical axis;

         1

   (ii) labelling the vertical axis;

         1

   (iii) plotting the remaining bars.

         1

(An additional grid, if needed, will be found on page 28.)

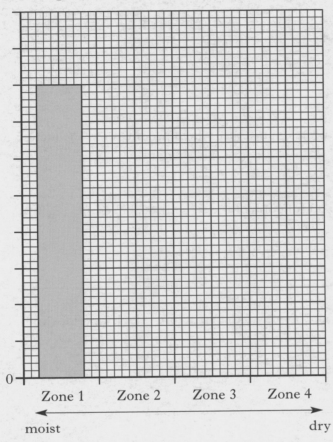

Zone 1   Zone 2   Zone 3   Zone 4

moist ←——————————→ dry

(b) (i) From the results in the table, describe the relationship between soil moisture and the percentage of seeds germinated.

_____

_____

         2

   (ii) Suggest how the investigators could tell whether a seed had germinated.

_____

         1

   (iii) Other than soil moisture, name **two** factors which are necessary for the germination of all types of seeds.

1 _____

2 _____

         1

Marks | KU | PS

3. (*a*) The diagram shows part of a honeysuckle flower.

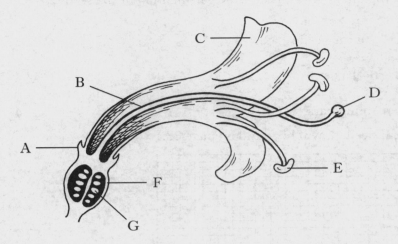

(i) Which letter indicates a structure which produces male gametes?

_____

1

(ii) Give the name and function of the structure labelled D.

Name _____

1

Function _____

1

(iii) Give the letter and name of the structure which develops into a fruit.

Letter _____

Name _____

1

3. (continued)

(b) (i) The diagram below shows stages in the life cycle of a flowering plant. Use words from the list to complete the diagram.

List: **fertilisation** **fruit formation** **pollination**

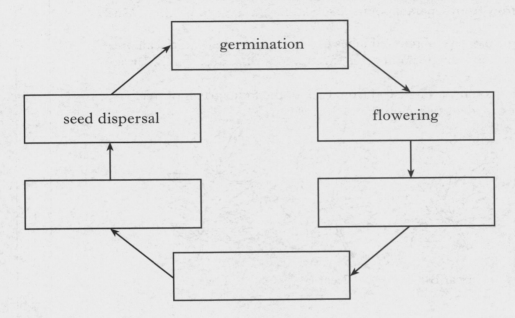

1

(ii) Underline **one** option in each set of brackets to complete the following sentence correctly.

The type of plant reproduction which involves seeds is $\left\{ \begin{array}{c} \text{sexual} \\ \text{asexual} \end{array} \right\}$

and cannot take place without $\left\{ \begin{array}{c} \text{insects} \\ \text{pollination} \end{array} \right\}$.

1

[Turn over

4. The key can be used to identify four species of trees from the shape of their leaves.

1   Leaf divided into a number of separate leaflets..........................Go to 2
    Leaf not divided into separate leaflets.......................................Go to 3

2   All leaflets grow from the same point ....Horse chestnut
    Leaflets grow from separate points ....Ash

3   Leaf outline has several pointed lobes ....Sycamore
    Leaf outline has a single point ....Lime

(a) The diagrams show a single leaf from each of the four species of tree. Use the key to identify each leaf.

Leaf A   Leaf B   Leaf C   Leaf D

_____   _____   _____   _____

2

(b) Use the same information from the key above to construct a branched key in the outline below.

(An additional outline, if needed, will be found on page 28.)

Tree Leaves

Leaf outline has several pointed lobes

Horse chestnut   _____   _____   _____

2

5. The table gives information about the nutrients found in 100 g of three different breakfast cereals.

	Cereal X	Cereal Y	Cereal Z
Protein (g)	15	10	15
Fat (g)	0	2	5
Carbohydrate (g)	60	65	65
Fibre (g)	10	15	5

(a) (i) Which cereal provides the most energy per 100 g?

Cereal _____

(ii) Calculate the protein : fat : carbohydrate content of Cereal X as a simple whole number ratio.

Space for calculation

____ : ____ : ____

protein : fat : carbohydrate

(iii) Which of the cereals is represented by the following pie chart?

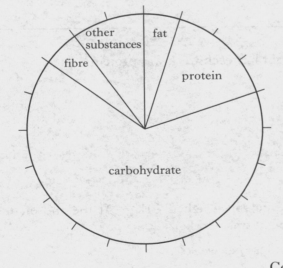

Cereal _____

(b) Animals obtain their energy from food.

Give **one** other reason why animals need food.

_____

(c) From which part of a mammal's digestive system are digestion products absorbed into the bloodstream?

_____

6. Loss of fat, protein and water all contribute to the total weight lost by a person on a slimming diet.

   The graph shows the changes in the percentages of these in the weight lost during a three week period.

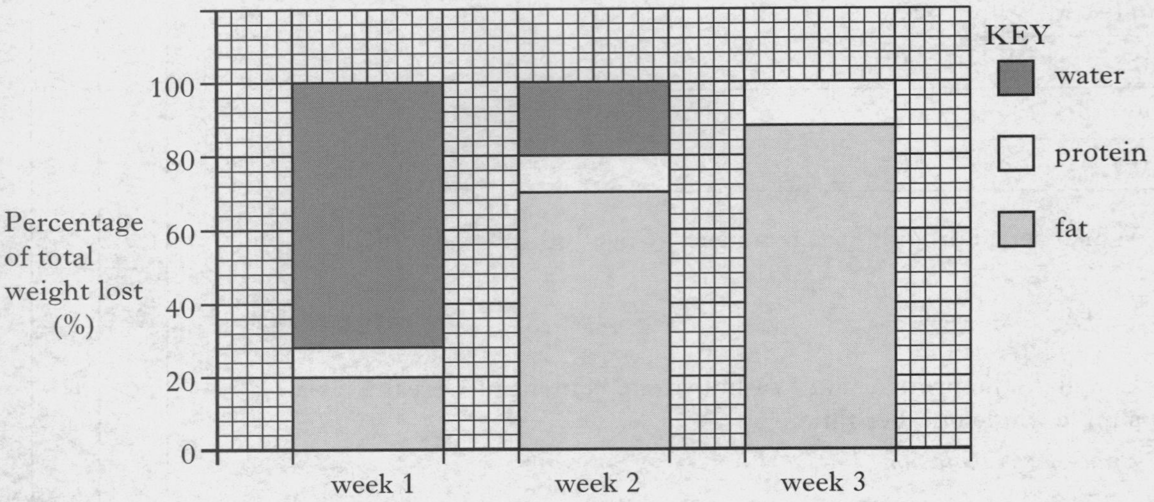

(a) During week 1, which substance accounted for most of the weight lost?

   _____

   1

(b) What happened to the percentage of fat in the weight lost by the person as the diet continued during the three weeks?

   _____

   1

(c) What percentage of the weight lost each week was protein?

   Week 1 _____%

   Week 2 _____%

   Week 3 _____%

   1

(d) Before starting the diet, the person weighed 70 kg. At the end of the three weeks, the person's weight was 62·5 kg.

   What was the average weight loss per week?

   Space for calculation

   _____ kg per week

   1

DO NOT WRITE IN THIS MARGIN

Marks KU PS

7. The graph shows the activity of enzymes A, B and C at different pH values.

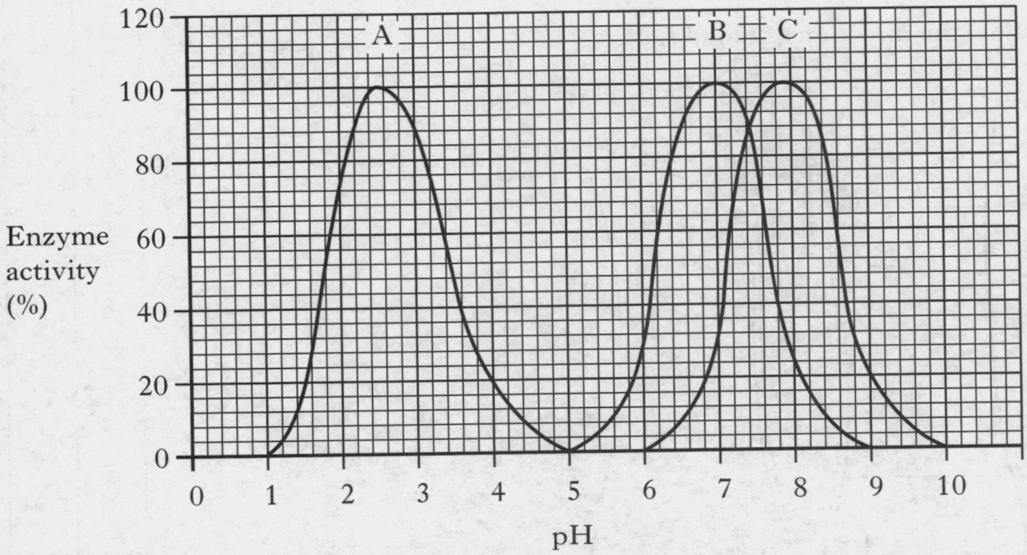

(*a*) Which enzyme could be pepsin?

Enzyme 1

(*b*) Over what pH range would enzymes B and C **both** be able to work?

Between pH _______ and pH _______ 1

(*c*) Describe the changes in the activity of enzyme B as the pH changes from pH 5 to pH 9.

____

____ 2

(*d*) (i) Enzymes are biological catalysts.

Explain the meaning of the word *catalyst*.

____

____ 1

(ii) What type of chemical substance are enzymes composed of?

_______________________________ 1

[Turn over

Marks | KU | PS

8. (*a*) The diagram below shows part of the system used to regulate water content in the human body.

The arrows show the direction of blood flow.

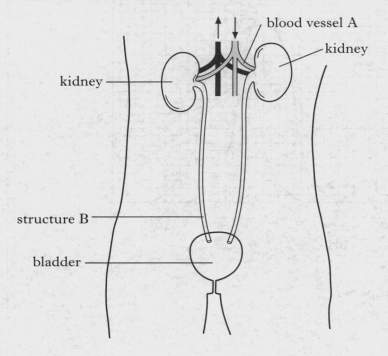

(i) Name blood vessel A.

_____

1

(ii) Name structure B.

_____

1

(iii) What is the function of the bladder?

_____

1

(iv) Name the toxic waste product removed from the blood by filtration in the kidneys.

_____

1

8. (continued)

(b) The table below shows the daily water gains and losses of a person at three different temperatures.

		Normal temperature	Colder temperature	Warmer temperature
Water gain (cm^3)	In drinks	1500	1500	1500
	In food	800	800	800
	From respiration	300	300	300
	TOTAL	2600	2600	2600
Water loss (cm^3)	In breath	400	400	600
	In sweat	1000	600	4000
	In urine	1100	1500	500
	In faeces	100	100	100
	TOTAL	2600	2600	

(i) Water balance is usually achieved by the body.

What evidence from the table supports this statement?

_____

1

(ii) What **two** differences are shown in the table between the body's responses to normal and colder temperatures?

1 _____

2 _____

1

(iii) Complete the table by calculating the missing total volume of water loss in the warmer temperature.

Space for calculation

1

(iv) How would water balance usually be achieved in the warmer temperature?

_____

1

[Turn over

9. (*a*) The diagram represents a leaf cell from a green plant.

(i) Complete the table by naming the parts of the leaf cell.

Label	Part of leaf cell
A	
B	
C	
D	

2

(ii) State the function of a cell nucleus.

_____

_____

1

(*b*) (i) Name **one** substance that can enter a cell by diffusion.

_____

1

(ii) A substance enters a cell by diffusion. What does this indicate about the concentrations of that substance inside and outside the cell?

_____

1

9. (continued)

(c) A microscope has a choice of three objective lenses. The total magnification depends on the magnifications of the eyepiece lens and the objective lens. Complete the table below to show the magnifications of the microscope.

Eyepiece lens magnification	Objective lens magnification	Total magnification
× 7	× 10	× 70
× 7		× 140
	× 40	× 280

1

(d) The table below gives information about the size of some cells.

Type of cell	Length of cell (micrometres)
red blood cell	7
human skin cell	20
Elodea leaf cell	80
onion epidermal cell	100

(i) Calculate the length of an onion epidermis cell in millimetres.
(1 millimetre = 1000 micrometres)

Space for calculation

_____ millimetres

1

(ii) Using information from the table, what general conclusion could be made when comparing animal and plant cells?

_____

1

[Turn over

Marks | KU | PS

10. Read the passage below.

Likeable Lichens

(adapted from Dobson, F., 2003, "Getting a Liking for Lichens", *Biologist*, 59, 263-267)

Lichens consist of two organisms, a fungus and an alga. Both gain benefit from the association. The fungus forms 90% of the mass of a lichen and provides support and protection. The alga is located in a thin layer just beneath the upper surface. Unlike the fungus, the alga can photosynthesise.

Lichens are found from the hottest desert rocks to the freezing polar regions. About eight percent of the land area of the world is frozen tundra and in such regions lichens are by far the most important photosynthetic organisms. If global warming was to cause a severe reduction in their numbers, the resulting increase of carbon dioxide in the air could be as dangerous to our survival as the loss of the rain forests.

Lichen species differ in their ability to tolerate air pollution. The presence or absence of certain lichens can be used to give a measure of sulphur dioxide levels. In recent years, the level of this pollutant has been falling. Sulphur dioxide emissions in Britain fell by 69% in the ten years from 1990 to 2000. In Kew Gardens in London, the number of species of lichens recorded rose from 6 to 76.

Yellow lichens placed on wounds were known to reduce the chances of infection and saved many lives after battles. It is now known that these lichens contain usnic acid, which has strong anti-bacterial properties. Several antiseptic creams have been produced commercially from this chemical but lichens grow too slowly for large-scale production. Work is proceeding to manufacture similar compounds synthetically.

(*a*) Which types of organism combine to form lichens?

_____   1

(*b*) Species which can give information about environmental factors are called "indicator species". Select a **complete sentence** from the passage which shows that lichens are useful in this way.

_____

_____

_____   1

(*c*) Suggest a benefit to the fungus from its association with the photosynthetic alga.

_____   1

DO NOT
WRITE IN
THIS
MARGIN

Marks | KU | PS

10. **(continued)**

(d) Calculate the average yearly increase in the number of lichen species present in Kew Gardens in the ten years from 1990 to 2000.

Space for calculation

Average increase = _____ species per year

1

(e) (i) What property of yellow lichens allows them to be used to prevent infections?

_____

1

(ii) What problem prevents the use of lichens for large-scale manufacture of medical products?

_____

1

[Turn over

Marks | KU | PS

11. The diagram shows part of the breathing system.

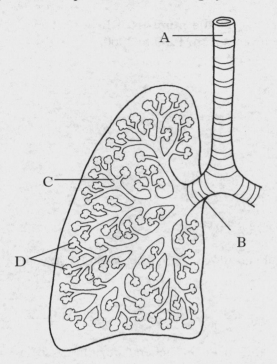

(a) Use letters from the diagram to complete the table below.

Structure	Letter
bronchus	
windpipe	
air sac	
bronchiole	

2

(b) Name the gas which passes from the blood into the lungs to be breathed out.

_____

1

Marks | KU | PS

11. (continued)

(c) In an investigation into breathing rates, a pupil had his number of breaths per minute recorded when exercising at different levels.

The procedure was repeated three times and the results are shown in the table below.

Exercise	Breathing rate (breaths per minute)			
	1st Trial	2nd Trial	3rd Trial	Average
standing still	16	15	17	16
walking	19	17	18	18
jogging	27	25	29	27
running quickly	33	31	32	32

(i) Calculate the percentage change in the average breathing rate when running quickly, compared to standing still.

Space for calculation

_____ % increase

1

(ii) What is the relationship between the level of exercise and breathing rate?

_____

_____

1

(iii) Why was the investigation repeated three times and an average calculated?

_____

1

[Turn over

Official SQA Past Papers: General Biology 2006

DO NOT
WRITE IN
THIS
MARGIN

Marks | KU | PS

12. The diagram shows part of the human ear.

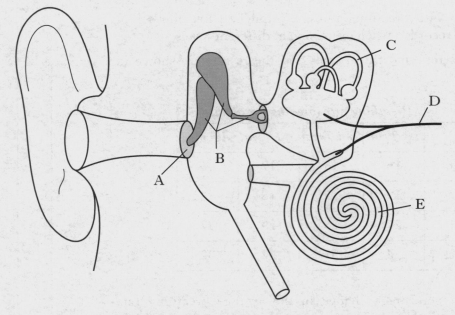

(a) Complete the table to show the name and function of the labelled parts.

Letter	Name	Function
A	ear drum	
	middle ear bones	pass vibrations to inner ear
C		detects movement of the head
		produces nerve signals
	auditory nerve	

3

12. **(continued)**

(*b*) In an investigation, a group of people were asked if they could hear a buzzer. This was repeated at different distances and the percentage of people hearing the buzzer was calculated. The results are shown in the table.

Distance from buzzer (m)	Percentage of people hearing buzzer
5	100
10	98
15	96
20	88
25	74
30	60

On the grid below, complete a **line graph** of the results by:

(i) labelling the horizontal axis; 1

(ii) adding an appropriate scale to the horizontal axis; 1

(iii) plotting the graph. 1

(An additional grid, if needed, will be found on page 29.)

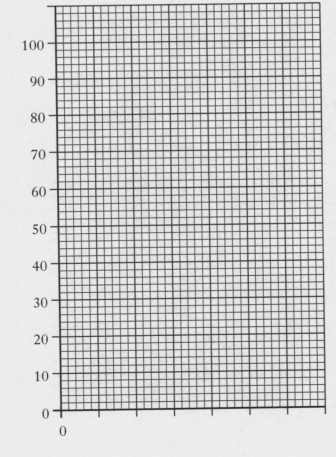

Percentage of people hearing the buzzer

Marks | KU | PS

13. (a) The skeleton provides protection for parts of the body.
Give **two** other functions of the skeleton.

1 _____

2 _____

1

(b) Use lines to link the parts of the skeleton to each of the organs of the body which they protect.

Part of skeleton   *Organs*

| rib cage | | heart |

                                 | brain |

| vertebrae | | lungs |

| skull | | spinal cord |

2

14. (*a*) The table below shows the change in the number of cases of three childhood diseases in a population.

	Number of cases		
Year	*Measles*	*Mumps*	*Rubella*
1997	700	180	700
1998	650	155	680
1999	450	150	430
2000	420	110	300
2001	330	90	230
2002	410	150	270

  (i) How many children suffered from Rubella in 1999?

  _____

  1

  (ii) Which disease always affected fewer children than the others?

  _____

  1

  (iii) What pattern in the number of cases is shown by all the diseases over the six years of the study?

  _____

  _____

  2

(*b*) Genetically engineered micro-organisms can be used to make products with medical value. Interferon, used in the treatment of some cancers, can be produced from reprogrammed bacteria, as can human growth hormone which is given to some children to treat pituitary dwarfism. Genetically engineered bacteria are used to produce insulin which is used to treat diabetes. Hepatitis is a liver disease which can be caused by a virus. A vaccine has been developed from genetically engineered yeast cells which helps prevent people becoming infected with the virus.

Complete the table to summarise this information.

Medical condition	Medical product	Type of genetically engineered micro-organism
cancer		
		bacteria
	vaccine	
	insulin	

2

Marks | KU | PS

15. (a) (i) Complete the diagram to show the sex chromosomes present in the cells of two generations of people.

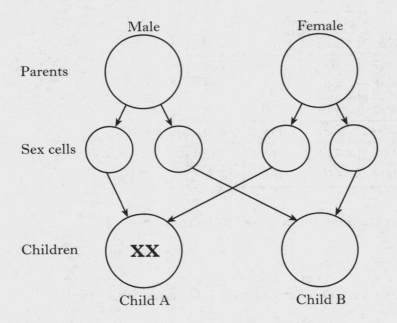

Male   Female

Parents

Sex cells

Children   **XX**

Child A   Child B

2

(ii) What is the sex of Child A?

_____

1

(b) (i) The statements below refer to human sex cells.

Use lines to connect each statement to the correct sex cell.

Statement   *Sex cell*

| released in large numbers |

| contains a large food store | | egg |

| produced by the male parent | | sperm |

| moves with the use of a tail |

2

(ii) What is the general name given to sex cells such as eggs and sperm?

_____

1

DO NOT
WRITE IN
THIS
MARGIN

Marks | KU | PS

15. **(continued)**

(*c*) How many complete sets of chromosomes are present in a sperm cell?

_____

1

(*d*) What name is given to each part of a chromosome which controls a particular characteristic?

_____

1

[Turn over

16. The diagram represents one type of sewage treatment works.

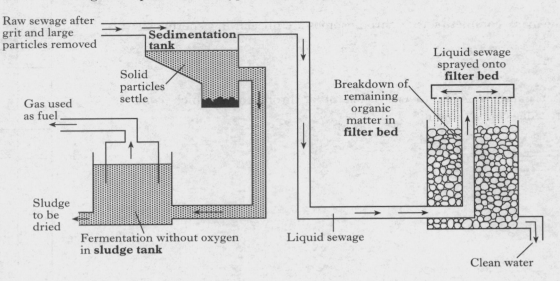

(a) What causes the breakdown of the organic matter in the filter bed?

_____ 1

(b) The filter bed contains layers of stones and gravel. How does this help to provide the oxygen needed for the breakdown of organic matter?

_____

_____ 1

(c) (i) Name the gas which is produced in the sludge tank and which can be used as a fuel.

_____ 1

(ii) State **one** advantage of using fuels obtained by fermentation rather than fossil fuels.

_____ 1

17. The pH of three different types of milk was measured. After 48 hours in a warm place, the pH was measured again. The results are shown in the table.

Type of milk	pH at start	pH after 48 hours
unpasteurised	6·9	4·2
pasteurised	7·0	5·9
ultra heat treated	6·9	6·0

The production of acid causes the milk to become sour.

(a) Which type of milk was the most sour after 48 hours?

_____

(b) Pasteurisation and ultra heat treatment kill bacteria in milk.

What effect do these processes have on the souring of milk?

_____

(c) Predict the pH of the pasteurised milk if it had been kept in a colder place for 48 hours.

Tick the correct box

☐ 7·5

☐ 7·0

☐ 6·4

☐ 5·5

(d) Underline one word in the brackets to complete the following sentence correctly.

Souring of milk is an example of a $\left\{ \begin{array}{l} \text{digestion} \\ \text{synthesis} \\ \text{fermentation} \end{array} \right\}$ reaction.

[END OF QUESTION PAPER]

[Turn over

Marks — KU — PS

1

1

1

1

SPACE FOR ANSWERS
AND FOR ROUGH WORKING

ADDITIONAL GRID FOR QUESTION 2(a)

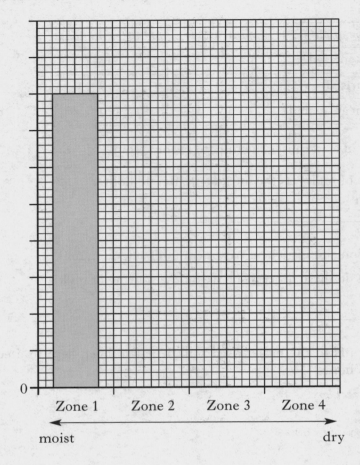

ADDITIONAL KEY OUTLINE FOR QUESTION 4(b)

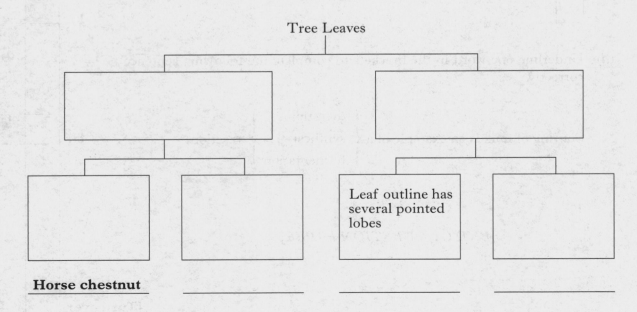

SPACE FOR ANSWERS
AND FOR ROUGH WORKING

ADDITIONAL GRID FOR QUESTION 12(*b*)

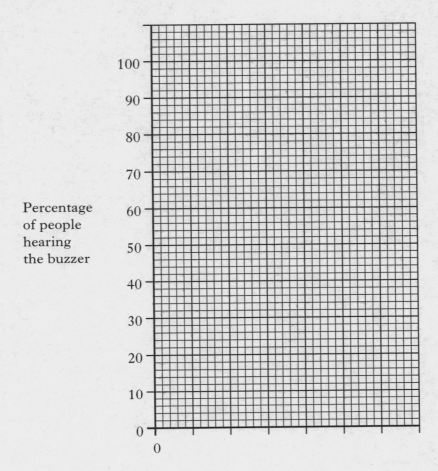

SPACE FOR ANSWERS
AND FOR ROUGH WORKING

[BLANK PAGE]

FOR OFFICIAL USE

G

KU	PS

Total Marks

0300/401

NATIONAL
QUALIFICATIONS
2007

MONDAY, 21 MAY
9.00 AM – 10.30 AM

BIOLOGY
STANDARD GRADE
General Level

Fill in these boxes and read what is printed below.

Full name of centre

Town

Forename(s)

Surname

Date of birth
Day Month Year

Scottish candidate number

Number of seat

1 All questions should be attempted.

2 The questions may be answered in any order but all answers are to be written in the spaces provided in this answer book, and must be written clearly and legibly in ink.

3 Rough work, if any should be necessary, as well as the fair copy, is to be written in this book. Additional spaces for answers and for rough work will be found at the end of the book. Rough work should be scored through when the fair copy has been written.

4 Before leaving the examination room you must give this book to the invigilator. If you do not, you may lose all the marks for this paper.

SCOTTISH
QUALIFICATIONS
AUTHORITY

©

LI 0300/401 6/32270

1. The diagram shows a food web from a moorland ecosystem.

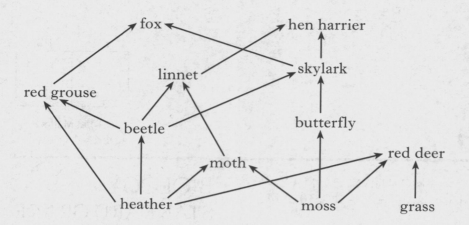

(*a*) The following statements refer to the food web.

Complete the table by entering "**T**" when the statement is true, and "**F**" when the statement is false.

Statement	*T or F*
Linnets are eaten by beetles and moths.	
Foxes and hen harriers are not eaten by anything.	
Butterflies are eaten by skylarks which are eaten by foxes.	

1

(*b*) Give an example of a producer and a consumer from the food web.

Producer _____

Consumer _____

1

(*c*) Which plant provides energy for the greatest number of different species in this food web?

_____

1

(*d*) Give **two** ways in which energy can be lost from this food web.

1 _____

2 _____

2

2. (a) The phrases below refer to man's influence on natural resources.

1. Overgrazing by too many animals in one area
2. Air pollution by sulphur dioxide released by burning fossil fuels
3. Overfishing by modern fishing boats

Choose **one** of the phrases and describe a problem which may result from it.

Phrase number _____

Problem _____

_____

1

(b) The diagram shows the position of a food-processing factory beside a river.

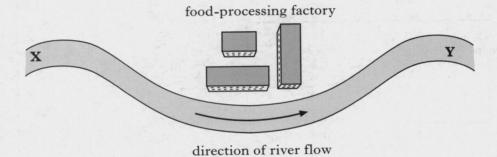

food-processing factory

X   Y

direction of river flow

The factory accidentally released organic waste into the river.

Water samples were taken from points **X** and **Y** and analysed for the numbers of micro-organisms and oxygen concentration.

(i) Complete the following sentence by <u>underlining</u> the correct word in each bracket.

Water samples from point **X** had $\begin{Bmatrix} more \\ fewer \end{Bmatrix}$ micro-organisms and a $\begin{Bmatrix} higher \\ lower \end{Bmatrix}$ oxygen concentration than samples from point **Y**.

1

(ii) What does the organic waste provide for the micro-organisms in the river?

_____

1

[Turn over

Official SQA Past Papers: General Biology 2007

DO NOT
WRITE IN
THIS
MARGIN

Marks | KU | PS

3. Some features of common seaweeds are shown in the table below.

Seaweed	Colour	Shape	Bladders
Bladder wrack	brown	branched	in pairs
Channel wrack	brown	grooved	absent
Cladophora	green	long and thin	absent
Egg wrack	brown	branched	along its length
Sea lettuce	green	flat	absent
Serrated wrack	brown	saw-toothed edges	absent
Spiral wrack	brown	twisted	in pairs

(a) (i) Use the information in the table to complete the key below by writing the correct feature on each dotted line and the correct seaweed names in the empty boxes.

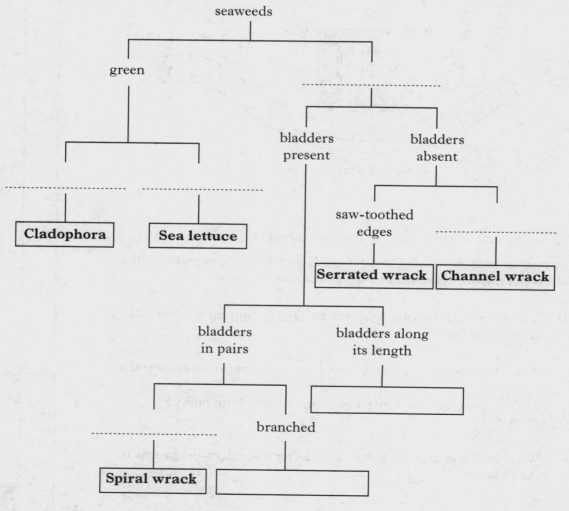

3

DO NOT WRITE IN THIS MARGIN

Marks | KU | PS

3. **(a)** **(continued)**

(ii) Describe **two** differences between Sea lettuce and Spiral wrack.

1 _____

2 _____   1

(iii) Describe the features which Bladder wrack and Spiral wrack have in common.

_____   1

(b) Abiotic factors can affect the community of seaweeds that grow on a rocky shore.

Identify **two** abiotic factors from the list below.

Tick (✓) the correct boxes

temperature ☐

competition ☐

light intensity ☐

grazing by limpets ☐

disease ☐   1

[Turn over

4. There are four major groups of plants. Features used to identify members of each group include the presence of a transport system, the shape of their leaves and their method of reproduction.

Flowering plants and the conifers reproduce using seeds. They both have transport systems but they differ in the shape of their leaves. Conifers have needle-like leaves whereas the leaves of flowering plants are either narrow or broad. Mosses don't have any true leaves or transport systems. Ferns have transport systems and feathery leaves but they reproduce using spores, as do the mosses.

(a) Use the information above to complete the table about the plant groups.

Plant group	Transport system	Leaves	Structures used in reproduction
	absent	no true leaves	
Ferns			spores
Conifers			seeds
	present	narrow or broad	

3

(b) One type of transport system in plants carries water from the roots to the leaves.

(i) Name the type of tissue involved in this transport system.

_____

1

(ii) Describe a function of a different transport system in plants.

_____

_____

1

(c) Some plants are useful to humans.

State a use by humans of a named plant.

Plant _____

Use _____

1

5. The diagrams show two natural methods of asexual reproduction in flowering plants.

Method A

Method B

Strawberry plant

Potato plant

(a) Name the two methods of asexual reproduction.

Method A _____

Method B _____   **2**

(b) What does structure **X** contribute to the growth of a new potato plant?

_____

_____   **1**

(c) Name an artificial method of propagating flowering plants.

_____   **1**

[Turn over

DO NOT WRITE IN THIS MARGIN

Marks KU PS

6. The chart shows the times when different vegetable crops can be sown and harvested.

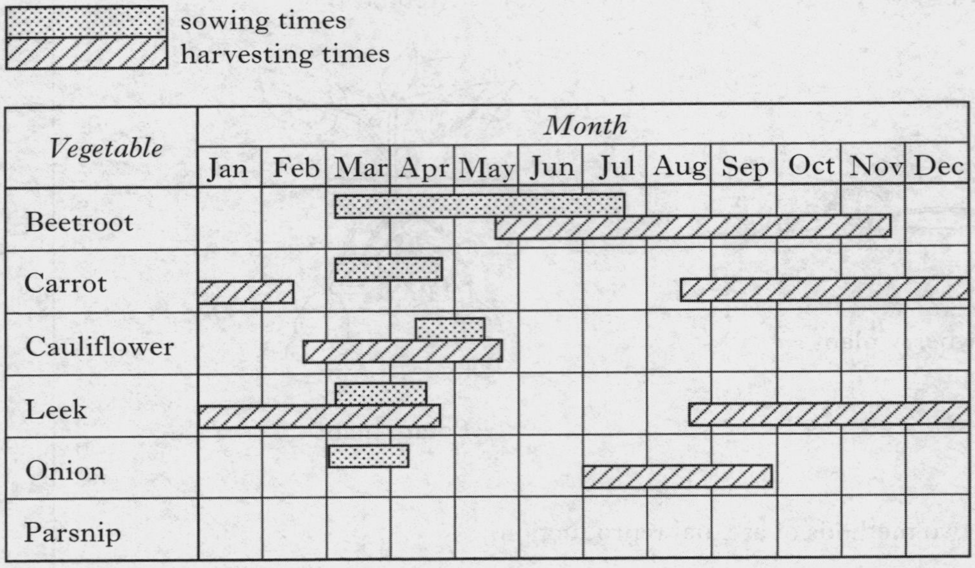

sowing times
harvesting times
Vegetable
Month
Jan Feb Mar Apr May Jun Jul Aug Sep Oct Nov Dec
Beetroot
Carrot
Cauliflower
Leek
Onion
Parsnip

(*a*) Parsnip seeds can be sown throughout March and April. The parsnip crop can be harvested from the beginning of November to the end of February.

Add this information to the chart. **2**

(An additional chart will be found, if needed, on page 28.)

(*b*) During which month is it possible to sow seeds for all the vegetables?

____________________ **1**

(*c*) Which crop can be harvested over the longest period of time?

____________________ **1**

(*d*) Name **all** the crops which could be harvested in the same month as seeds of the same species are being sown.

____ **1**

7. (*a*) An investigation was set up to examine the behaviour of slugs.

Food

During the investigation the slugs moved towards the food.

(i) Two possible hypotheses for the movement of the slugs are:

1 The slugs saw the food and moved towards it.

2 The slugs smelled the food and moved towards it.

How could the investigation be improved to show which hypothesis was correct?

_____

_____ 1

(ii) Why was it good experimental practice to use several slugs rather than just one?

_____ 1

(*b*) Give **one** example of an abiotic factor which can affect the behaviour of a named animal and describe the response of the animal to that factor.

Animal _____ Abiotic factor_____ 1

Response _____

_____ 1

[Turn over

Marks | KU | PS

8. (a) The diagram shows the skulls of two mammals.

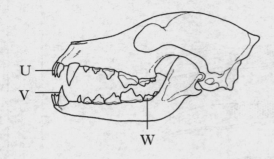 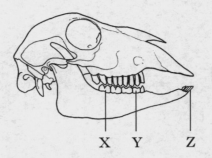

Use letters from the diagram to identify the following teeth.

(i) Incisors _____ and _____   **1**

(ii) A tooth used for piercing and holding prey _____   **1**

(iii) A tooth used for crushing and grinding plant material

_____   **1**

(b) The diagram below shows the human digestive system.

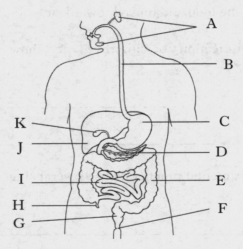

(i) Complete the table to identify the following parts of the digestive system.

Part of digestive system	Letter
oesophagus	
pancreas	
	K
	C

2

DO NOT WRITE IN THIS MARGIN

Marks KU PS

8. (*b*) (continued)

(ii) What is the main function of part E of the diagram?

____ 1

(*c*) The diagram shows a cross section of the small intestine.

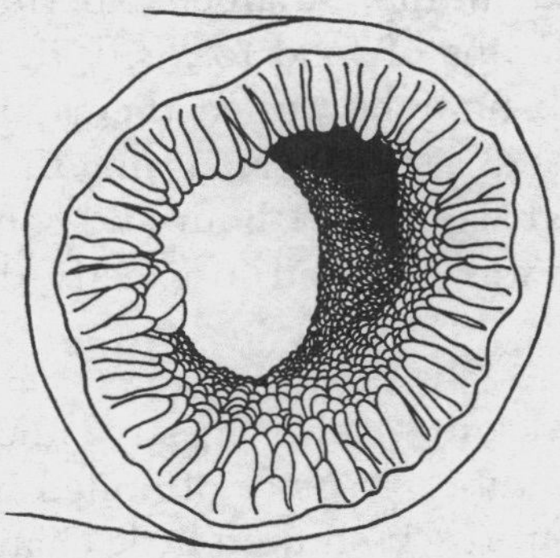

Describe **one** feature of the small intestine shown on the diagram and explain how it helps in the absorption of food.

Feature ____

Explanation ____

____ 1

[Turn over

DO NOT
WRITE IN
THIS
MARGIN

Marks | KU | PS

9. Read the following passage and answer the questions based on it.

Alexis St. Martin – Human Guinea Pig

In 1822, a 20 year old Canadian fur trapper called Alexis St. Martin was accidentally injured by a shotgun. His abdomen and stomach were blasted open. He survived thanks to prompt treatment by a local doctor. His stomach did not fully heal and Alexis was left with an opening to his stomach which the doctor covered with a leather flap.

The doctor was a keen scientist and carried out more than 60 experiments on his patient. In one experiment he tied lumps of food to a silk thread and pushed them into Alexis' stomach. Each hour he pulled them out to see what the stomach juices had done to the food, carefully recording the results. A piece of boiled beef was half the original size after 1 hour and completely gone after 2 hours. A piece of raw beef was digested in exactly the same manner.

In another experiment, the doctor removed some of the digestive juices from Alexis' stomach and put them into a glass tube. A piece of boiled beef was put into the tube and kept at body temperature. It showed little change after 1 hour, was only half gone in 2 hours and disappeared after 4 hours.

Despite his injuries Alexis led a long and healthy life. He married and had six children. He survived to the age of 86, outliving the doctor by many years.

(a) What was the purpose of the silk thread?

_____

_____ 1

(b) Why did the doctor keep the experiment in the glass tube at body temperature?

_____

_____ 1

(c) How long did Alexis live after the shotgun accident?
Space for calculation

_____ years 1

9. (continued)

(*d*) Use information from the passage to complete the table of results.

		Raw beef in stomach	*Boiled beef in stomach*	*Boiled beef in glass tube*
Time (hours)	0	unaffected	unaffected	unaffected
	1			
	2			
	4		digestion complete	digestion complete

2

[Turn over

Marks | KU | PS

10. (*a*) (i) What effect does cell division have on the number of cells in the human body?

_____

1

(ii) What part of a cell controls cell division?

_____

1

(*b*) The following phrases describe stages in cell division.

Stage P—Chromosomes line up at the equator of the cell.

Stage Q—Nuclear membranes form and cytoplasm divides.

Stage R—Chromatids separate and move to opposite ends of the cell.

Stage S—Each chromosome doubles itself and appears as coiled threads.

Use the letters to arrange the stages into the correct order.

First stage   _____

Second stage   _____

Third stage   _____

Fourth stage   _____

1

(*c*) A cell divides every 20 minutes. How many cells would be produced from one original cell at the end of two hours?

Space for calculation

_____ cells

1

11. The graph shows the maximum recommended pulse rate for humans of different ages.

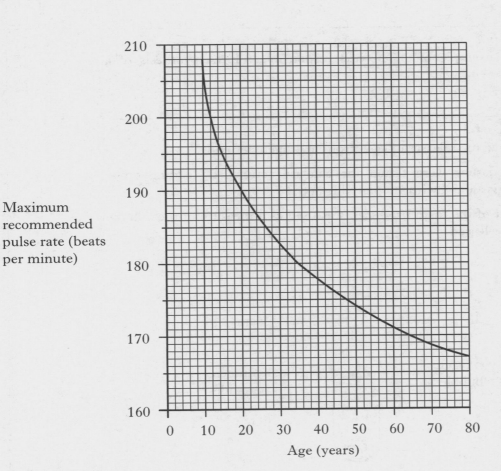

(a) What is the maximum recommended pulse rate for a person aged 15 years?

_____ beats per minute

1

(b) At what age does the maximum recommended pulse rate fall below 200 beats per minute?

above _____ years

1

(c) Calculate the percentage decrease in the maximum recommended pulse rate between the ages of 20 and 60 years.

Space for calculation

1

_____%

12. (a) All living cells require enzymes. What would happen to chemical reactions in a cell if enzymes were not present?

_____

1

(b) Give **one** example of an enzyme responsible for the synthesis of a substance.

_____

1

(c) Catalase enzyme releases oxygen from hydrogen peroxide.

Different tissues were tested for catalase activity by adding equal masses of tissue to hydrogen peroxide at pH 7.

The height of the foam produced was used as a measure of the volume of oxygen released.

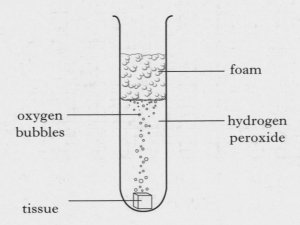

The results are shown in the table.

Type of tissue	Height of foam (mm)
apple	24
potato	28
beef	53
carrot	22
fish	48
chicken	50

(i) Give **one** variable, other than pH, which must be kept constant in this investigation.

_____

1

Marks | KU | PS

12. *(c)* **(continued)**

(ii) Use the information in the table to complete the bar chart by:

1 adding a scale to the *y*-axis; **1**

2 labelling the *y*-axis; **1**

3 drawing the bars. **1**

(An additional grid will be found, if needed, on page 28.)

Type of Tissue

(iii) Beef, fish and chicken tissues produced greater volumes of oxygen than the others.

Suggest a hypothesis which could explain this fact.

_____

_____ **1**

(iv) The investigation was carried out at pH7.

Use the words **increase**, **decrease** or **stay the same** to complete the following sentence correctly.

At pH 4 oxygen production would_____ and

at pH 11 oxygen production would _____ . **1**

[Turn over

13. (*a*) The diagram shows part of a human skeleton.

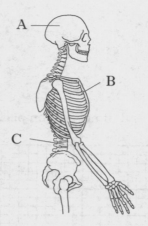

A

B

C

Complete the table below to name each part of the skeleton labelled on the diagram and name **one** organ protected by that part.

Letter	Part of skeleton	Organ protected
A		
B		
C		

2

(*b*) Complete the table below by inserting ticks (✓) to say whether each line refers to a hinge joint, a ball and socket joint or both types of joint.

	Hinge	Ball and socket
shoulder joint		
knee joint		
hip joint		
elbow joint		
can move in only one plane		
can move in many planes		
held together by ligaments		
cartilage protects the ends of the bones		

3

Marks | KU | PS

13. (continued)

(*c*)   The diagram shows some of the muscles in a human leg.

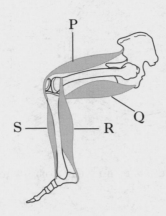

(i)   Which muscle contracts to straighten the leg?

_____

1

(ii)   What is the name of the structures which attach the muscles to bones?

_____

1

[Turn over

Marks | KU | PS

14. (a) The diagram shows a human eye.

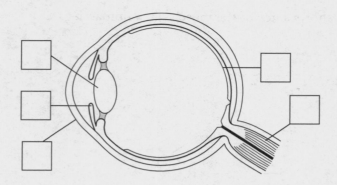

Use the information in the table below to add the correct letters to the diagram.

Letter	Description
A	cornea
B	optic nerve
C	controls the amount of light entering the eye
D	changes shape to adjust focus
E	converts light to electrical impulses

2

(b) The diagram shows an investigation into the judgement of distance.

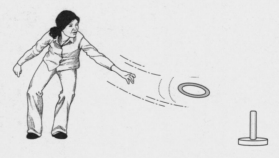

Volunteers each threw 10 hoops at a peg 3 metres away. The number of successful throws was recorded. Each volunteer attempted the test three times, once using the right eye only, once using the left eye only and once using both eyes.

The results are shown in the following chart.

14. *(b)* **(continued)**

⬚ right eye only   ■ left eye only   ▨ both eyes

Number of successes per ten throws

(i) Calculate the average number of successful throws by the volunteers for each trial.

Space for calculations

Average number of successful throws using right eye only _____ .

Average number of successful throws using left eye only _____ .

Average number of successful throws using both eyes _____ .

2

(ii) Suggest **two** valid conclusions about the distance judgement of the volunteers which can be drawn from the results.

1 _____

_____

2 _____

_____

2

(iii) The brain, spinal cord and nerves are all involved in such activities. What is the collective name for these parts of the body?

_____

1

15. (a) The diagrams below show the inheritance of the sex chromosomes **X** and **Y**.

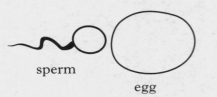

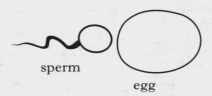

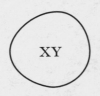

Sex _____   Sex _____

Complete the diagrams by:

(i)   inserting the missing sex chromosomes into the eggs and sperm;   **1**

(ii) writing the sex of each fertilised egg in the spaces provided.   **1**

(b) Complete the following sentences by <u>underlining</u> the correct word in each bracket.

The name given to a group of interbreeding organisms which produce

fertile young is a $\left\{ \begin{array}{l} \text{tissue} \\ \text{clone} \\ \text{species} \end{array} \right\}$.

Characteristics of offspring are controlled by $\left\{ \begin{array}{l} \text{enzymes} \\ \text{genes} \\ \text{phenotype} \end{array} \right\}$.   **2**

(c) (i)   Down's Syndrome is an example of a condition caused by a change to the chromosomes.

What is the correct term for a change to the chromosomes?

_____   **1**

(ii) Down's Syndrome can be detected before birth by the removal of some of the fluid surrounding the baby as it develops. The fluid is removed by a doctor using a syringe inserted into the uterus.

What name is given to this procedure?

_____   **1**

Official SQA Past Papers: General Biology 2007

DO NOT
WRITE IN
THIS
MARGIN

Marks | KU | PS

15. (continued)

(d) The following table shows the risk to women of different ages of having a
baby with Down's Syndrome.

Woman's age (years)	Risk of Down's Syndrome (per 10 000 births)
18	4
22	6
28	8
32	12
38	34
42	100

(i) How many times greater is the risk to a 42 year old woman of having
a Down's Syndrome baby, compared to an 18 year old woman?
Space for calculation.

_____ times greater

1

(ii) Complete the line graph below by:

1   completing the scale on the *y*-axis;

1

2   adding a label to the *y*-axis;

1

3   plotting the graph.

1

(An additional grid will be found, if needed, on page 29.)

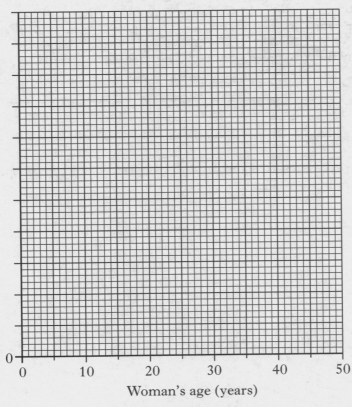

Woman's age (years)

Official SQA Past Papers: General Biology 2007

DO NOT
WRITE IN
THIS
MARGIN

Marks | KU | PS

16. In an investigation into the conditions required for making yoghurt, the following steps were carried out.

1   Milk was pasteurised by heating to over 75 °C.

2   Yoghurt-making bacteria were added to the milk and the mixture was stirred.

3   Four samples were taken and kept at different temperatures.

4   The pH of each sample was measured every hour.

The results are shown in the following table.

Temperature (°C)	pH of sample					
	Start	1 hour	2 hours	3 hours	4 hours	5 hours
5	7·0	7·0	7·0	7·0	7·0	7·0
20	7·0	6·8	6·5	6·0	5·4	4·8
35	7·0	6·5	5·9	5·2	4·4	3·5
50	7·0	7·0	7·0	7·0	7·0	7·0

(a) (i)   What precaution was taken to ensure that no harmful bacteria were present in the milk at the start?

_____

1

(ii)   From the results, what is the optimum temperature for yoghurt production?

_____°C

1

(iii)   Explain why the mixture kept at 50 °C did not change in pH.

_____

_____

1

(iv)   Name the process carried out by the bacteria which causes the milk to change into yoghurt.

_____

1

16. **(continued)**

(b) The table shows how the fat content of the yoghurt varies according to the type of milk used to make it.

Type of milk used	Fat content of yoghurt (%)
whole	over 3·0
semi-skimmed	0·5–3·0
skimmed	under 0·5

The following table shows the fat and lactose content of three yoghurts.

Yoghurt	Composition	
	fat (%)	lactose (%)
A	2·8	3·9
B	4·0	4·5
C	0·4	3·0

(i) Using information from both tables, identify which yoghurt was made from:

1 semi-skimmed milk   yoghurt _____

2 whole milk   yoghurt _____   **1**

(ii) What is the range of lactose concentrations in the yoghurts?

From _____ to _____%   **1**

[Turn over

DO NOT WRITE IN THIS MARGIN

Marks KU PS

17. (*a*) The following bar chart shows the incidence of diabetes in people of different ages.

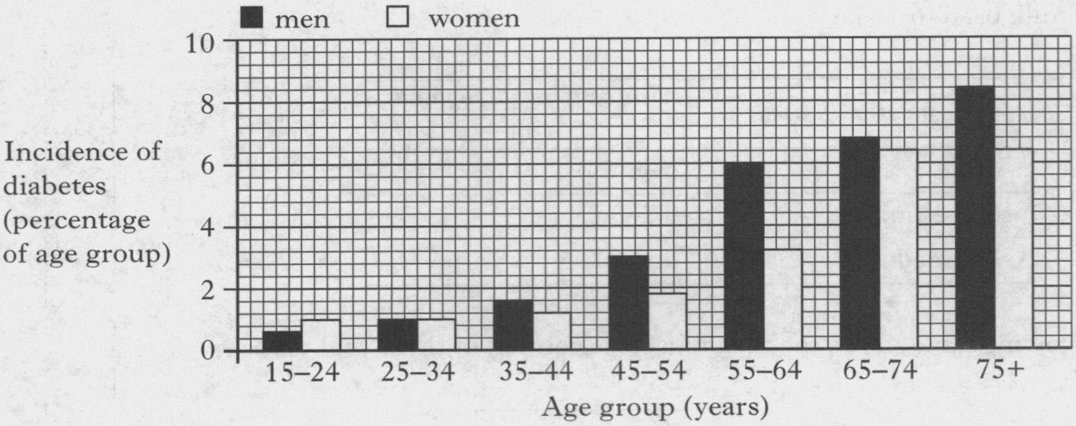

(i) Which age group has the highest incidence of diabetes?

____________ years **1**

(ii) What is the incidence of diabetes in the following groups?

A men aged between 35 and 44 ___________ %

B women aged between 55 and 64 ___________ % **1**

(iii) What age group shows no difference in the incidence of diabetes in men and women?

____________ years **1**

(*b*) (i) Diabetes can be treated with a substance produced by genetic engineering. Name this substance.

________________________________ **1**

(ii) What type of chemical, used in biological washing powders, can be produced by genetic engineering?

________________________________ **1**

(iii) During genetic engineering, what is transferred into bacteria from another organism?

________________________________ **1**

Official SQA Past Papers: General Biology 2007

DO NOT
WRITE IN
THIS
MARGIN

Marks | KU | PS

18. The eye colours of 160 school pupils are shown in the table below.

Eye colour	Number of school pupils
brown	80
green	24
blue	48
grey	8

(*a*) Complete the pie chart to show this information.
(An additional chart will be found, if needed, on page 29.)

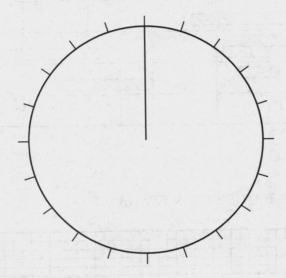

(*b*) What type of variation is shown by eye colour?

_____

(*c*) What percentage of the school pupils had green eyes?
Space for calculation

_____%

[*END OF QUESTION PAPER*]

2

1

1

SPACE FOR ANSWERS
AND FOR ROUGH WORKING

ADDITIONAL CHART FOR QUESTION 6(a)

| | sowing times |
| | harvesting times |

Vegetable	Month											
	Jan	Feb	Mar	Apr	May	Jun	Jul	Aug	Sep	Oct	Nov	Dec
Beetroot			sowing			harvesting						
Carrot	harvesting		sowing					harvesting				
Cauliflower			harvesting		sowing							
Leek	harvesting		sowing					harvesting				
Onion			sowing			harvesting						
Parsnip												

ADDITIONAL GRAPH PAPER FOR QUESTION 12(c)(ii)

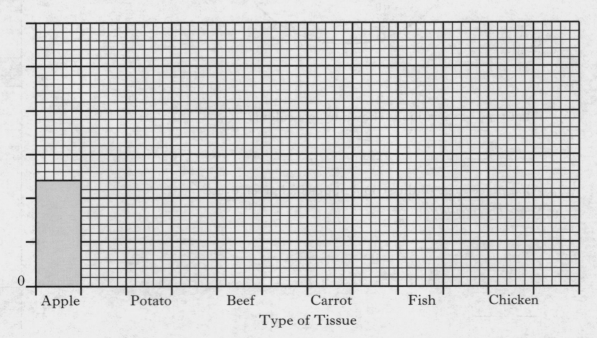

Type of Tissue

SPACE FOR ANSWERS
AND FOR ROUGH WORKING

ADDITIONAL GRAPH PAPER FOR QUESTION 15(*d*)(ii)

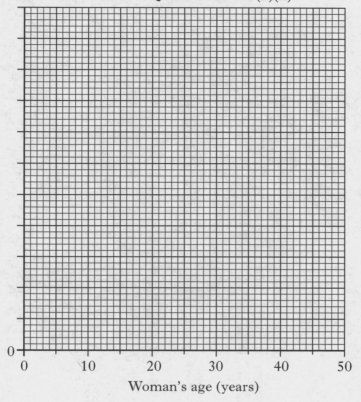

Woman's age (years)

ADDITIONAL CHART PAPER FOR QUESTION 18(*a*)

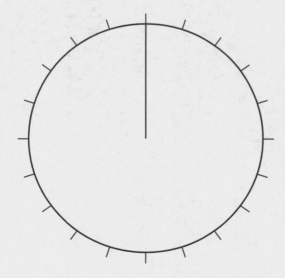

SPACE FOR ANSWERS
AND FOR ROUGH WORKING

SPACE FOR ANSWERS
AND FOR ROUGH WORKING

[BLANK PAGE]

[BLANK PAGE]

[BLANK PAGE]

[BLANK PAGE]

[BLANK PAGE]

[BLANK PAGE]

Acknowledgements

The following companies have very generously given permission to reproduce their copyright material free of charge: *The Herald* for the article 'Stirring Stuff's in the Bag' (2004 paper p 16).

Pocket answer section for
SQA General Biology
2003 to 2007

Published by Leckie & Leckie Ltd, 3rd Floor, 4 Queen Street, Edinburgh EH2 1JE
tel: 0131 220 6831, fax: 0131 225 9987, enquiries@leckieandleckie.co.uk, www.leckieandleckie.co.uk

Biology General Level 2003

1. (a) Food web

   (b) (i) Producer – oak tree
       Consumer – woodlice/beetles/worms/
       squirrels/spiders/hedgehogs/blackbirds/
       foxes/hawks
       (ii) transfer of energy
       (iii) oak leaves ➜ beetles ➜ spiders ➜
       hedgehogs ➜ foxes
       (iv) acorns
       (v) leaves

   (c) • habitat = where an organism lives
       • population = all the animals or plants of a
       single species living in an area
       • ecosystem = a particular area and all the
       animals and plants which live there

2. (a) 13 000

   (b) (i) A
       (ii) C = carbon monoxide
       D = smoke

3. (a) 2·8

   (b) 50

   (c) decreases (or equivalent) … increases (or
   equivalent)
   (d) B smaller decrease in oxygen concentration/
   increase in oxygen concentration begins
   sooner/oxygen concentration downstream
   (from B) is higher (than from A)/oxygen
   concentration recovers sooner

   (e) typhoid/cholera/polio/dysentery

4. (a) (i) Found at the very back of the jaw   A
       Known as an incisor   C
       Used for grinding and crushing food   A
       (ii) killing prey/gripping (food)/(tearing) food

   (b) (i) 3
       (ii) 4
       (iii) 1. greater protection/more effective/fewer
       decayed teeth
       2. same protection with lower
       concentration/fewer side effects/less
       expense/avoids using excess fluoride

5. (a) (i) breath/breathing/exhaling
       (ii) 150
       (iii) 20

   (b) kidneys

   (c) urea

5. (continued)

(d)
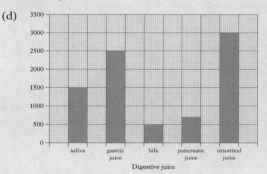

(e) large intestine/colon

6. (a) (i) stomata/stoma
       (ii) carbon dioxide
       (iii) water

   (b) starch

   (c) chlorophyll

7. (a) (i) B and C
       (ii) A

   (b) B graft/grafting
   D tubers

8. (a)
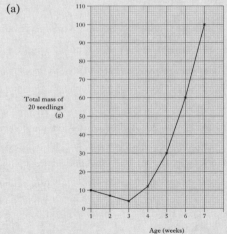

   (b) (i) 3
       (ii) ✓ 6–7 weeks
       (iii) 5

Biology General Level 2003 (cont.)

8. (c) (i) Any two from:
temperature/light/water/nutrients/type of
soil/type of container/soil pH/humidity/
planting depth/seed spacing

   (ii) increases reliability/reduces effect of
individual variations/to make sample or
results representative

   (iii) removing excess water/drying

   (d) no increase in mass/continued loss in mass

9. (a) cytoplasm   ✓
nucleus   ✓
cell membrane   ✓

   (b) make them easier to see/increase visibility,
clarity, contrast/to make parts of the cells easier
to see/to make parts of the cells visible because
cells are transparent

   (c) 120

10. (a) W glucose
X oxygen
Y water

   (b) food

   (c) Any two from:
heat/growth OR
repair/transport/movement/cell division OR
mitosis

11. (a) (i) 44
   (ii) 6

   (b) Water molecules moved into the funnel ✓

   (c) any value in range 84–90

12. (a) Middle East yoghurt is more acidic and thinner

   (b) skimmed (milk)/evaporated (milk)/dried (milk)

   (c) kill bacteria/reduce growth OR activity of
bacteria

   (d) lactic (acid)

   (e) heating (to 85–95°C)/Pasteurisation

   (f) slower bacteriagrowth/fermentation/production
of lactic acid slower bacterial activity

   (g) increase in acidity

13. (a) (i) 1. gold (body)   2. black (body)
   (ii) black (body)
   (iii) 4:1

   (b) All the F_1 generation have the
same genotypes and phenotype   ✓

   (c) discontinuous

   (d) gametes

14. (a) movement/muscle attachment/support/makes
blood cells/framework for body

   (b) (i) Ligament
   (ii) protects bones/cushions bones/shock
absorber/reduces friction/allows smooth
movement/stops bones rubbing together

   (c)
Range	Type	Example
one plane	hinge	knee/elbow/finger/toe
many planes	ball and socket	hip/shoulder

15. (a) (i) B
   (ii) for comparison/to show that one factor is
causing an effect/to show there is no
carbon dioxide in unbreathed air/to show
that the breathed air contains the carbon
dioxide

   (b) Any two from:
   • volume/amount of air breathed OR rate of
breathing or number of breaths/how long
air is breathed in and out
   • volume/amount of indicator
   • concentration of indicator/
   • colour OR pH of indicator
   • temperature
   • pupil

16. (a)
The chamber that receives blood from the body	A
The artery that carries blood from the heart to the body	F
The chamber that pumps blood to the lungs	C
The vein that carries blood from the lungs to the heart	G

   (b) red blood cells
plasma

17. (a) genetic engineering OR genetic modification
OR reprogramming microbes

   (b) insulin – treat diabetes/
growth hormone – treat growth problems/
Factor VIII – treating haemophilia/
interferon – cancer treatment

   (c) asexual/binary fission

18. (a) pneumonia and skin abscesses

   (b) grow as single cells, spiral shaped cells, cause
Lyme's disease

   (c) E. coli

Biology General Level 2004

1. (*a*) (i)

Consumer	Diet
Moths	**ferns, trees**
Ground-living insects	grass
Voles	**ferns, tree-living insects**
Weasels	mice, voles
Tree-living insects	trees
Shrews	tree-living insects, mites
Fungi	trees
Mites	**fungi**
Spiders	ground-living insects
Owls	**mice, voles, shrews**

(ii) ferns → moths → mice → weasels / owls

(*b*) Producer - something which makes food / carries out photosynthesis / gets its energy from the sun.

Consumer – something which eats / feeds off / gets its energy from other organisms / organic matter

2. (*a*)

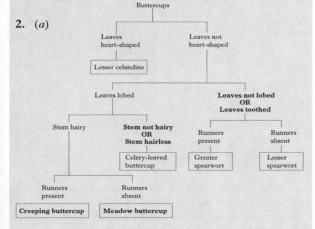

(*b*) leaf shape / one has heart-shaped leaves / one has toothed leaves

lesser celendine has heart-shaped leaves / lesser spearwort has toothed leaves

(*c*) leaf shape **and** absence of runners / both have lobed leaves **and** no runners

3. (*a*) (i)

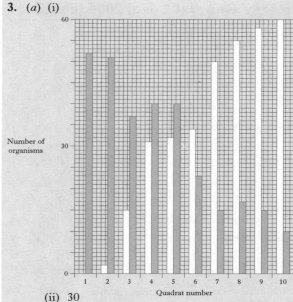

(ii) 30

(iii) increasing / rising

(*b*) increase in numbers / increased population

(*c*) water temperature, salt concentration

(*d*) habitat / abiotic factors

4. (*a*) (i) B
carbon dioxide has not been removed

(ii) oxygen

(iii) so new starch could be detected / existing starch would prevent new starch being detected / so any starch found must have been made during the investigation / to see which plant can now make starch

(iv) species / type / size / age / health / leaf area / leaf number

(*b*) stoma / stomata / stomal pores

(*c*) chlorophyll

(*d*) (i) **A** sepal
(ii) **E** stigma
(iii) **F** ovary

5. (*a*) (i) **J** oviduct / fallopian tube
K uterus / womb
L ovary

(ii) Eggs produced   **L**
Fertilisation takes place   **J**
Fertilised egg becomes attached **K**

Biology General Level 2004 (cont.)

5. (*b*)

Statement	Eggs	Sperm
Contain a food store for developing fetus	✓	
Swim using a tail		✓
Produced in testes		✓
In most fish, are deposited into the water	✓	✓
Are g014 gametes	✓	✓

6. (*a*) Humidity / moisture (in the air) / water vapour

(*b*) They settle in the humid / moist area OR
They move to the humid / moist area OR
They move away from the dry area OR
They move to the side with water.

(*c*) To allow them to settle / to allow them to explore conditions / to allow them to adjust to conditions / to allow them time to move.

(*d*) To get a reliable / representative result
One may have been unreliable / unrepresentative / atypical

(*e*) Light / temperature

(*f*) 1. Make both sides the same humidity / put water in both sides / put drying agent in both sides / make the bottom the same on both sides / take out the water and the drying agent.
2. Cover / shade one side OR shine light on one side

7. (*a*)

Leaf cell	Cheek cell
A B C D E	A D E

(*b*) (i) Iodine solution + acetic orcein
(ii) Turns cytoplasm pink
(iii) Acetic orcein

(*c*) Stain

(*d*)

Power	Eyepiece lens magnification	Objective lens magnification	Total magnification
Low	× 12	× 4	**× 48**
Medium	× 12	× 10	**× 120**
High	× 12	**× 40**	× 480

8. (*a*) (i) 2
(ii) Diffusion

(*b*) (i) Water
(ii) (+) 20
(iii) 0.4
(iv) 0.25

9. (*a*) (about) 135 million cups

(*b*) Relaxation

(*c*) Heart disease

(*d*) Lung, bowel, digestive system

(*e*) Tannin, caffeine

(*f*) Any three of: Organic, Chai spice, decaffeinated, herbal, iced

10. (*a*) 102

(*b*) Colour

(*c*) 20

11. (*a*) (i) It doubles
(ii)

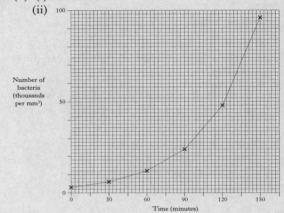

(iii) 768

(*b*) 1st stage **C**
2nd stage **B**
3rd stage **D**
4th stage **A**

(*c*) In comparison with the original cell, the number of chromosomes present in a cell produced by mitosis is **the same** and it contains **the same** information.

12. (*a*)

Letter	Name of structure	Function
A	**Cornea**	Allows light to enter the eye
B	**Lens**	**Focuses light/ Produces a clear image**
C	Iris	**Controls amount of light entering / size of pupil**
D	**Retina**	Converts light into electrical impulses
E	Optic nerve	**Carries nerve signals / impulses / information**

12. (*b*) **Sight** – judgement of distance / 3D vision
   Hearing – judgement of direction of sound

   (*c*) (i) Muscles / effectors / glands
   (ii) 1 Brain
       2 Spinal cord

13. (*a*) (i) (Bone) marrow and lymph nodes
   (ii) White (blood cells)
   (iii) Red (blood cells)
   (iv) Protein
   (v) Engulf bacteria and produce antibodies
   (vi) 7200 million

   (*b*) (i) Capillary
   (ii) **H** – anywhere in blood vessel
       L – anywhere in muscle cells

   (*c*) Red blood cell / RBC / haemoglobin /
   oxyhaemoglobin

14. (*a*) They are different species

   (*b*) (i) Red

   (ii)

Generation	Symbol
A	P
B	F_1
C	F_2

   (iii) 4:1

15. (*a*) (i) Both have the thalassaemic gene
   (ii) Parents have affected children

   (*b*) 50% / half / 1 in 2 / 2 out of 4 / 1 to 1

   (*c*) Amniocentesis

16. (*a*) glucose / sugar → alcohol / ethanol + carbon
   dioxide + energy

   (*b*) 1. Making alcohol
   2. Baking

   (*c*) Yeast is a fungus and is single-celled

   (*d*) 1. Wash with disinfectant / wash with alcohol /
   cover with sterile material
   2. Flame / heat it till its red hot / put it in a
   bunsen

   (*e*) Prevent contamination (with unwanted
   microbes) / prevent escape of microbes /
   prevent escape of spores

Biology General Level 2005

1. (*a*) (i) movement/flow/transfer of energy
   (ii) 3
   (iii)

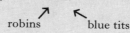

   hawks
   robins   blue tits
       woodlice

   (*b*) (i) woodlice numbers increase / more
   woodlice + less food for beetles / increased
   competition
   (ii) birth rate greater than death rate / death
   rate less than birth rate
   (iii) increase / increase in birth rate / decrease
   in death rate

   (*c*) micro-organisms
   nutrients
   plants

2. (*a*) 1

   (*b*) (i) A   embryo
       B   food store
   (ii) seed coat

   (*c*)

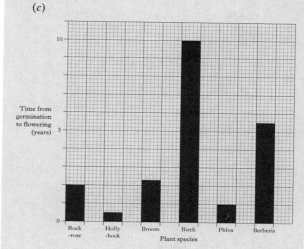

3. (*a*) 3376   4459
   (*b*) 278
   (*c*) 65

4. (*a*) chlorophyll
   (*b*) phloem
   (*c*) carbon dioxide and water
   (*d*) starch

5. (*a*) cover / shade one side

   (*b*) (i) humidity / moisture / temperature
   (ii) humidity / moisture – Put moist cotton
       wool / water or equivalent in base of
       one side. Put equivalent dry
       material / drying agent / nothing in
       other side

Biology General Level 2005

5. *(b)*(ii) (continued)

temperature - Surround one side with ice pack or equivalent. Surround other side with warm material

6. *(a)*   to make the results reliable / representative reduce effect of atypical result

(b)   144

(c)   reaction time decreases

7. *(a)*   A→D→C→B→E

(b)

Letter	Name	Function
B	ovary	produces / stores / releases eggs or female sex cells
C	uterus / womb	where the embryo develops
E	testis / testes / testicle	produces / releases sperm or male sex cells

(c) (i) yolk sac / egg yolk
(ii) by parents / adults

8. *(a)* (i) W   Z
(ii) S
(iii) P   Q

(b)   left ventricle pumps blood further

(c) (i) arteries —— away from the heart

veins   through the tissues

capillaries   towards the heart

(ii) arteries

9. *(a)*

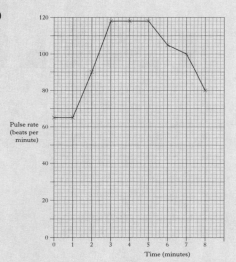

(b)   pulse rate higher than start/pulse rate had not returned to normal/pulse rate still above 65

(c)   continue timing until pulse rate returns to normal /65 / starting rate

(d)   shorter/faster

10. *(a)*   it releases excess histamine

(b)   common for members of the same family to be affected / to have hayfever

(c)   wheezy chest

(d)   early summer

(e)   steroids

(f)   can cause serious side effects / they can only be given under close hospital supervision

11. *(a)* (i) discontinuous
(ii) 200

(b) (i)

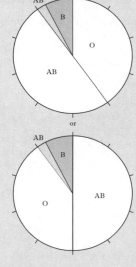

(ii) 40%

(c) (i) Similarity - group AB lowest (in both) / group B 3rd (in both)
Difference - group O largest in X, not in Y / group A largest in Y, not in X
(ii) Y
larger sample size

12. *(a)*   23

(b)   increases
increases

(c)   decrease / moves slower

13. *(a)*   A

(b)   Longer for starch to be produced / less starch produced / longer to change colour

(c) (i) phosphorylase / enzyme alone will not produce starch / phosphorylase + G-1-P needed for starch production
(ii) glucose −1-phosphate alone will not produce starch / phosphorylase + G-1-P needed for starch production

14. *(a)* (i) breakdown
(ii) synthesis
(iii) synthesis

14. (*b*)   protein

(*c*)   muscle contraction   cell division

15. (*a*)   (i) F
(ii) A
(iii) B+I
(iv) E
(v) C

(*b*)   (i) 2
(ii) 7

16. (*a*)

Improvement	Explanation
oxygen inlet below surface	increased oxygen availability to bacteria / reduce waste of oxygen
thermometer bulb below surface	improved temperature measurement / to get temperature of the liquid
cooling jacket/ heating mechanism/ insulation	maintain (optimum) temperature
stirrer	spread oxygen / heat / nutrients / cells

(*b*)   (i) aerobic
(ii) food / nutrients / glucose / heat
(iii) carbon dioxide
(iv) heat

17. (*a*)   (i) methane / biogas / fuel / fertiliser
(ii) micro-organisms / bacteria / fungi / protozoa / microbes
(iii) (biological) filtration / filter bed / trickle / spray sewage over stones / air spaces in filter beds
activated sludge process / bubble air through sewage /
stirring sewage

(*b*)   (i) January, February, March, November, December
(ii) temperature

18. (*a*)   50

(*b*)   carbon dioxide

(*c*)   Y

(*d*)   Z

(*e*)   fungus

19. (*a*)   air / atmosphere + land / soil / earth

(*b*)

Source	Example of pollutant
Industry	smoke / SO_2 / chemical waste / radioactive waste / oil / CO_2 / fumes / oxides of nitrogen / soot / nuclear waste / CO / noise / hot water / heavy metals /greenhouse gasses
agriculture / farming	fertilisers
domestic / people / household	litter

(*c*)   improved exhaust systems (or eg) / lead free petrol / traffic control measures (or eg) / increased use of public transport / electric vehicles / less harmful petrol/less use of cars/increase road tax

Biology General Level 2006

1. (a) (i) A and E any order
    (ii) B
    (iii) F

   (b) a group of individuals of the same species

   (c) (i) 5
       (ii) Several measurements added together
            Total divided by number of measurements taken
       (iii) Factor: soil moisture
             Reason: Ling found at moisture levels of 5 units or less, Bell found at 5 units or more
       (iv) Several quadrat positions should be used
            Quadrat positions should be made randomly
            Plants in quadrat recorded

2. (a)

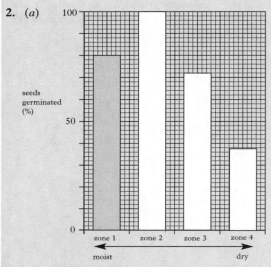
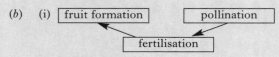

   (b) (i) As soil moisture increases up to 70 cm³ per 100 g, percentage germination increases. Above this, percentage germination decreases
       (ii) Appearance of root / shoot
       (iii) 1.   suitable temperature
             2.   oxygen

3. (a) (i) E
       (ii) Name: stigma
            Function: receives pollen
       (iii) Letter F
             Name ovary

   (b) (i) fruit formation ← fertilisation ← pollination

       (ii) sexual
            pollination

4. (a) Leaf A: Lime
       Leaf B: Sycamore
       Leaf C: Horse chestnut
       Leaf D: Ash

   (b)

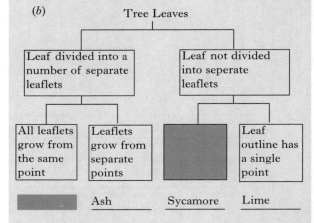

5. (a) (i) Z
       (ii) 1:0:4
       (iii) Z

   (b) growth / repair / cell division

   (c) small intestine / villi

6. (a) water

   (b) increased

   (c) Week 1   8
       Week 2   10
       Week 3   12

   (d) 2.5

7. (a) A

   (b) 6 and 9

   (c) Increases to maximum at pH7
       Then decreases

   (d) (i) It speeds up a chemical reaction
            It is unchanged after the reaction
       (ii) protein

8. (a) (i) renal artery
       (ii) ureter
       (iii) store urine
       (iv) urea

   (b) (i) Water gain = water loss in normal conditions
       (ii) In colder temperatures: water loss in sweat decreases and water loss in urine increases
       (iii) 5200
       (iv) Increase volume of drink

9. (a) (i) A   cell wall
            B   vacuole
            C   nucleus
            D   cytoplasm
       (ii) controls cell activities

9. (b) (i) oxygen / carbon dioxide / glucose / amino acids / water / salts / sugar

(ii) Higher concentration outside cell / Lower concentration inside cell

(c)

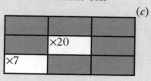

(d) (i) 0.1

(ii) Plant cells are larger than animal cells

10. (a) fungus and alga

(b) The presence or absence of certain lichens can be used to give a measure of sulphur dioxide levels

(c) It receives food

(d) 7

(e) (i) anti-bacterial / antiseptic / contains usnic acid

(ii) slow growth rate

11. (a) bronchus   B
windpipe   A
air sac   D
bronchiole   C

(b) carbon dioxide

(c) (i) 100

(ii) as the level of exercise increases, breathing rate increases

(iii) increases reliability of results

12. (a)

		vibrates in response to sound / passes vibrations to middle ear
B		
	semi-circular canals	
E	cochlea	
D		carries signal to brain

(b)

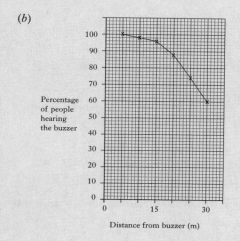

Distance from buzzer (m)

13. (a) *Any two of:*

1. provides support
2. allows movement / muscle attachment
3. makes blood cells

(b)

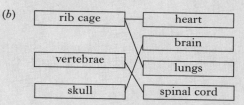

14. (a) (i) 430

(ii) Mumps

(iii) decrease until 2001 then increases in 2002

(b)

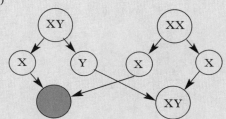

	interferon	bacteria
pituitary dwarfism	human growth hormone	
hepatitis		yeast
diabetes		bacteria

15. (a) (i)

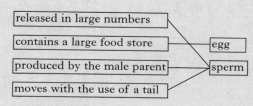

(ii) Female

(b) (i)

released in large numbers	
contains a large food store	egg
produced by the male parent	sperm
moves with the use of a tail	

(ii) gametes

(c) one

(d) gene

16. (a) micro-organisms / bacteria / fungi

(b) Provides air spaces / provides large surface area in contact with air

(c) (i) methane / biogas

(ii) renewable / reduces use of fossil fuels / produces less SO_2

17. (a) unpasteurised

(b) reduces / slows

(c) 6.4

(d) fermentation

Biology General level 2007

1. (a)   F
             T
             T

     (b) Producer: heather, moss or grass
        Consumer: red grouse, beetle, moth, butterfly, red deer, linnet, skylark, hen harrier or fox

     (c) heather

     (d) *Any two of:*
        heat, movement, decomposition/uneaten remains, faeces or migration from habitat

2. (a)   1. loss of plants, starvation of animals, reduced biodiversity, soil erosion or desertification
          2. acid rain: damages trees or plants or lichens, causes damage to buildings, causes breathing problems, makes streams, etc, more acidic, kills aquatic animals
          3. fish stocks reduced, fish populations destroyed, some species may become extinct, food sources for some other animals are reduced, upsets food webs or food chains

     (b) (i) fewer
          higher
       (ii) *Any one of:*
          food, energy, nutrients

3. (a) (i)

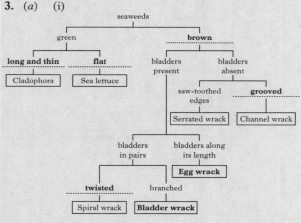

       (ii) *Any two of:*
          Sea lettuce is green, Spiral wrack is brown.
          Sea lettuce is flat, Spiral wrack is twisted.
          Sea lettuce does not have bladders, Spiral wrack does
       (iii) both are brown, both have bladders in pairs

     (b)   temperature, light intensity

4. (a)

Mosses	absent	no true leaves	**spores**
Ferns	**present**	**feathery**	spores
Conifers	**present**	**needle-like**	seeds
Flowering plants	present	narrow or broad	**seeds**

     (b) (i) xylem
       (ii) transports sugar or glucose or food or nutrients or products of photosynthesis

     (c) Any suitable example and appropriate use

5. (a)   **A** runners
          B tubers

     (b) food, starch, sugar, glucose, energy, materials for new cells or genetic information

     (c) cuttings, grafting, layering, tissue culture

6. (a)

	J	F	M	A	M	J	J	A	S	O	N	D
Parsnip		▨	●●●●									▨

     (b)   April

     (c)   Leek

     (d)   Beetroot, Cauliflower and Leek

7. (a) (i) Place food out of sight while still allowing scent to reach slugs, place food in an unsealed container or behind a screen
          OR
          Keep food in sight while preventing scent reaching slugs, place food in a transparent sealed container, replace food with replica food
       (ii) reduce effect of atypical result/reduce the effect of individual variation/improves reliability

     (b) Any named animal, appropriate factor and appropriate response, e.g. woodlouse, moisture/humidity: moves towards moist areas/higher humidity or moves away from dry areas/low humidity

8. (a) (i) U and Z
       (ii) V
      (iii) X or Y

     (b) (i)

oesophagus	**B**
pancreas	**D**
gall bladder	K
stomach	K

       (ii) absorb/reabsorb water

     (c) Villi or many small projections create large surface area/increase rate of absorption.
       OR
       Large surface area increases rate of absorption.

9. (*a*) To pull food from stomach

(*b*) To provide optimum temperature for digestion, to keep the experiment conditions similar to the body

(*c*) 66

(*d*)

Time	Raw beef in stomach	Boiled beef in stomach	Boiled beef in glass tube
0	unaffected	unaffected	unaffected
1	half gone, half digested or half original size	half gone, half digested or half original size	little change
2	all gone, all digested, digestion complete	all gone, all digested, digestion complete	half gone, half digested or half original size
4	all gone, all digested, digestion complete	digestion complete	digestion complete

10. (*a*) (i) increases/rises
(ii) nucleus

(*b*) S, P, R, Q

(*c*) 64

11. (*a*) 195

(*b*) 12

(*c*) 10

12. (*a*) slow down, stop

(*b*) phosphorylase

(*c*) (i) temperature, mass/volume of tissue, surface area of tissue
concentration/volume of H_2O_2
diameter of tube or time in solution (Any one)

(ii)

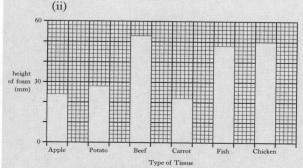

(iii) Animal/meat tissue contains more catalase than plant tissue, animal catalase more active than plant catalase, tissues with more protein contain more catalase

(iv) decrease
decrease

13. (*a*)

Letter	Part of skeleton	Organ protected
A	Skull/cranium	brain
B	ribs/rib cage	heart/lungs
C	spine, backbone, vertebrae or spinal column	spinal cord

(*b*)

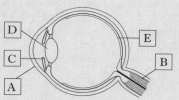

	Hinge	Ball and socket
shoulder joint		✓
knee joint	✓	
hip joint		✓
elbow joint	✓	
can move in only one plane	✓	
can move in many planes		✓
held together by ligaments	✓	✓
cartilage protects the ends of the bones	✓	✓

(*c*) (i) P
(ii) tendons

14. (*a*)

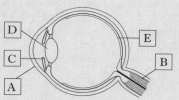

(*b*) (i) 3
2
6

(ii) *Any two of:*
Better/easier with both eyes rather than one or not as good with one eye as with two.
Better/easier with right eye than with left or not as good with left eye as with right.
People differ in ability.

(iii) the nervous system

15. (*a*)

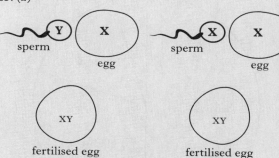

Sex   **male/man**   Sex **female/woman**

(*b*) species
genes

(*c*) (i) mutation
(ii) amniocentesis

Biology General level 2007 (cont.)

15. (d)   (i)   25

        (ii)

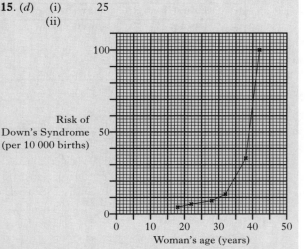

16. (a)   (i) milk was pasteurised/heated to over 75°C

        (ii) 35

        (iii) enzymes were denatured or bacteria were killed

        (iv) fermentation/anaerobic respiration

   (b)   (i) 1.   A

           2.   B

        (ii) 3·0 to 4·5

17. (a)   (i) 75+/ over 74/75 and over

        (ii) 1.   1·6

            2.   3·2

        (iii) 25-34

   (b)   (i) insulin

        (ii) enzymes/digestive enzymes

        (iii) chromosomal material/genes

18. (a)

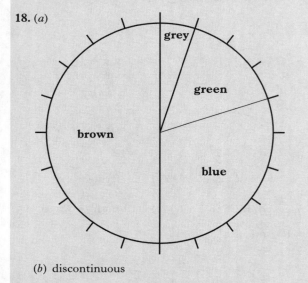

   (b) discontinuous

   (c) 15%